MERG

Peter Lion

D1554375

Published in the United States of America by

TFE Publishing
www.TFEPublishing.com
email: info@TFEPublishing.com

I am the living bread which came down from heaven: if any man eat of this bread, he shall live for ever: and the bread that I will give is my flesh, which I will give for the life of the world.

–John 6:51

(Inscription behind the altar of St. Mauritius Church, Eschweiler, Luxembourg)

To the men of the 28th Cavalry Reconnaissance Troop
(Mechanized),
the 28th Infantry Division
and all those who served.

Roll On!

One

Ghosts walk these roads and roam the patchwork fields blanketing this bucolic landscape. Blurs and shadows wandering through the misty forested hills and beyond. This is the feeling one gets while passing through the Ardennes foothills, a sense of a rich and painful history decades old yet remarkably palpable. Shadows calling your attention, demanding you feel their presence, calling on you to remember what happened here and their right to be here. Hoping that you won't forget.

Here the paragraphs and photographs from countless history books, the newsreel films that captured a war fought in black and white, the battles won, the ground gained, the goals achieved, the lives lost and the reasons why, come to vivid life. Driving these roads, walking past these fields or hiking these woods one sees and feels that now seemingly not so distant past. You fail to notice driving more slowly than you usually might. Scanning the countryside you feel unease; an expectation. Something moved in those shadows, there along the distant tree line. Probably just wind and leaves. Probably. A quick glance at the rearview mirror. Rounding that same bend in the road, just as you had moments ago, coming into view now the front of…a truck. The mind plays tricks. Just a truck.

In the distance long, sleek, white propellers glint in the midday late autumn sun while turning a slow, steady rhythm, marking their own passage of time. They are spurred by a warm breeze that rolls over the verdant valley, seeking the comfort of the cool pine-forested hills of the Luxembourg countryside. Randomly placed it seems, the turbines stand a silent sentinel over stone and hedge bordered fields that effortlessly slip away from both sides of the road, reaching east and west to the horizons. Stretches of this road, that gently weaves along the foothills of the Ardennes forest, are lined with trees stripped of leaves weeks ago where Northern Goshawks perch, waiting. A flash of wings, a sudden dive; talons sharp and sure finding prey. This is the only sign of conflict now along this road, one of several winding away from the town of Clervaux, a storybook town nestled in the deep, narrow Clerf River valley in the northern part of the country. Clervaux is an ideal blend of past and present and has long been the epitome of a vacation retreat. Of the past, the 12th century castle, severely damaged during WWII but now restored and housing among other things a war museum, perches majestically on a rocky bluff overlooking the present: souvenir shops, restaurants, hotels, cafés and bars lining worn cobblestone streets. At separate times during the war Clervaux served as a retreat for battle-weary soldiers of both sides but it wasn't until December 1944 that town's strategic importance became clear.

In the overcast pre-dawn hours of December 16th, 1944 a heavy artillery barrage along an 80 mile front in the Ardennes forest stretching from Belgium through Luxembourg, thinly protected by battle-fatigued American troops in this the "quiet sector" signaled the beginning of Germany's last major offensive of the war. The Germans officially called it the "Unternehmen Wacht am Rhein" ("Operation Watch on the Rhine") or the Von Rundstedt Offensive after the field marshal charged with overseeing and planning the attack. The French called it Bataille des Ardennes ("Battle of the Ardennes") while the official Allied military name was the Ardennes Counteroffensive. It was only after the Germans pushed westward deep into allied held territory creating a 50-mile salient in the battle lines that the news media coined the name that stuck: the Battle of the Bulge.

The German plan was loosely founded on the blitzkrieg (lightning war) attacks at the start of the war in May, 1940. British and French commanders had shored up defenses along the Maginot line, a series of concrete fortifications, obstacles and weapon placements constructed by the French after the First World War along its borders with Switzerland, Germany and Luxembourg. Named after the French Minister of war Andre Maginot, the fortifications were designed to give the French army time to mobilized should the Germans ever consider another attack, believing that the Germans would once again resort to the static trench warfare from two decades earlier. However Germany's new blitzkrieg strategy called for their armies to bypass the Maginot line altogether, instead attacking France through the "low countries" of Netherlands, Belgium and Luxembourg just north of the line. While a German attack along the northern shoulder of the line was not unexpected and troops were deployed in defense, it was in the thickly forested Ardennes regions of Luxembourg and Belgium that the French and British armies were at their weakest. The Germans exploited this weakness, attacking through the formidable terrain of the Ardennes forest, catching the defending armies off guard, and driving a wedge between the French and British armies that would ultimately see the battered British army retreating to the sea at Dunkirk and bring about France's surrender a few weeks later.

This time around the German attack was focused solely in the Ardennes and relied heavily on the elements of surprise, timing and winter weather, all crucial to the Germans in achieving their objective: to drive a wedge between the American and British armies while racing to capture the Belgian port of Antwerp. If they succeeded the Germans hoped this last great counter-offensive would destabilize the Allied efforts in Europe, ensnare massive numbers of Allied forces, prolong the war and the pending Allied advance into Germany and eventually achieve a negotiated peace, at least in the west. Success, Adolf Hitler believed, would also allow the Germans to move a majority of their forces eastward along the Russian front as well as allow Germany more time to design and produce advanced weaponry.

The attack indeed took the Americans by surprise. Even as it escalated Allied command simply couldn't believe that the Germans were capable of striking in such force. In the early stages of the assault, on the northern and southern flanks, American front line troops held their ground with tenacious and heroic fighting, thereby delaying critical elements of the German advance. In the middle sectors however, swiftly moving German tanks and infantry overwhelmed their enemy and pushed through. With two bridges wide enough and strong enough to support rapidly advancing armor and troops, the Germans knew taking Clervaux would allow access to *this road*, a relatively flat, straight, paved road leading south and west through the otherwise steep hills of the Ardennes forest to the town of Bastogne in neighboring Belgium. Bastogne was a key objective in the German battle plan. Capturing the crossroads town would give the Germans control of a crucial transportation hub allowing their attack to bypass the bottlenecks of the hilly, narrow, country back roads.

The attack would eventually penetrate deep into Belgium, creating the now famous bulge in the battle lines. However as the new year approached the Allies began to counter against the German advance, once again turning the tide of battle. The Wehrmacht began pulling back, retreating to Germany and by late January the battle front had returned to where it had been prior to the "Bulge". By that time however the American forces that had taken the brunt of the attack suffered 89,500 casualties including 19,000 killed, 47,500 wounded and 23,000 missing. For their part, German casualties were even higher with estimates ranging between 60,000 and 125,000 while approximately 3000 civilians were killed during the fighting.

Along this road now, signs point the way to monuments and memorials marking places of battle, honoring those who fought here and those who never left; signs guiding travelers to destinations now familiar with names marking their place in history: "St. Vith",

"Wiltz", "Bastogne"; and signs showing the names of destinations less known, yet vying for their claim on this county's past. Due south from Clervaux and just four miles north of Wiltz is one such sign, its black lettering on a bright yellow background declaring: "Eschweiler 4km".

This Luxembourg road is officially Route 328 and winds around the Ardennes foothills, cleaving eastward through stands of towering pines and hardwoods before leading to open pastures as the town nears. This is farming country and always has been. Highland cows and horses wander fields worked by families who have farmed here for generations. Approaching Eschweiler, homes sturdy and practical toe the road. They are typical of Luxembourg countryside with their traditional gray-black slate shingled roofs topping weathered but colorful stucco walls built on stone and brick foundations. These homes and farm buildings cling to a prideful past amongst newer, sleeker structures, boasting the latest architectural designs and materials that mark the present and eye the future. A map-dot town with a population of around three hundred people, Eschweiler was at one time a commune of neighboring Wiltz until 2015 when the two municipalities merged. So small is Eschweiler that one could easily drive into town from one end and be out the other end before you knew you'd been there, had it not been for the sharp bend in this narrow road at the center of town. At the outer elbow of the bend sits the small, modest church of Saint Mauritius.

While the parish of Eschweiler dates back to the 10th century, construction of the present-day church began in 1870 and it was consecrated on May 26, 1877. The only church in Luxembourg named after St. Mauritius, the patron saint of soldiers, sword smiths, armies, and infantrymen, it too is typical of the Luxembourg style. Rising from a gray stone foundation are gleaming white exterior walls spaced with oak rimmed, round-arched, stained glass windows. The sharply angled black slate roof covers a building twice as long as it is wide. At the front of the church, stone steps lead to the heavy, arched, dark brown oak doors of a small vestibule jutting out from the apsidal cathedral flanked, charcoal gray facade. One of the unique features of St. Mauritius is the round-cornered, square steeple and spire towering above the altar at the back of the church, rather than above the choir and organ in front as is typical. However it is when visitors step through the front doors and into the glass enclosed vestibule that they realize the simple features of the church exterior belie what awaits inside. There visitors are met by even more remarkable features: the saturated colors of the stained glass windows aglow from the light streaming in; the high arched ceiling vaulting above an ornately carved wooden altar and the richly painted mural adorning the wall behind the altarpiece. Perhaps the most obvious feature is the one that greets visitors the moment they enter the vestibule. On the wall to the left is the reason why here in Eschweiler, and in the surrounding towns and well beyond, the church of St. Mauritius is also and best known as the church of Mergenthaler.

TWO

When German forces invaded Luxembourg in May of 1940, Luxembourg itself ceased to to exist. Germany considered the people of Luxembourg ethnic Germans and as such they had "Heim ins Reich" (Home into the Reich) thereby justifying annexation rather than occupation. Initially under military rule, Nazi officials took up the administration of the country in July and began implementing a series of new laws meant to aide the process of "Germanizing" the population. Important administrative positions were handed out to German nationals and soon the Nazi Party was in control of all aspects of social and family life. Luxembourg was officially renamed "Gau Moselland" (the country district) with German now the official language. Teaching or even speaking the country's native language of "Lëtzebuergesch" was outlawed. Official government documents were now written in German. French and non-German sounding surnames were changed to German surnames thereby erasing, at least on paper, thousands of family histories. All street signs and government buildings were now named after high ranking Nazi party officials: gone was the "Grand Rue" of a given town, instead renamed "Adolf Hitler Strasse", "Hermann Goering Allee" or "Himmler Platz". Gone too were local customs, traditions and holidays not sanctioned by the new Nazi authority. Both manual and industrial workers were forced to join the Deutsches Arbeits Front (DAF) or face dismissal. Not long after assuming control, the Nazis began rounding up the small but vibrant Luxembourg Jewish population of about 3,500, many of them refugees from Germany who had fled west to escape Nazi persecution, and sending them east to various concentration camps. By October of 1941, the entire country was declared "judenrein" ("cleansed of Jews") except for those who remained in hiding. By the end of the war, only 36 people of the entire Jewish population of Luxembourg had survived.

In August of 1942, conscription into the Wehrmacht for all males of military age was introduced, an act that included swearing of an oath of allegiance to Adolf Hitler. Most had no choice but to enter into the German army to fight against the Allies and most of those fought on the Russian front. Those who refused service saw their families sent to forced labor camps, their property seized and in many cases handed over to displaced German families. Others went into hiding with some joining the small but dedicated resistance movement. As the end of August neared the people of Luxembourg, remembering their national motto "Mir woelle bleiwe waat mir sinn" (We want to remain what we are), turned their anger into action by organizing a general strike against their Nazi rulers. It began in the town of Wiltz, when on August 31, 1942 two town officials, Michel Worré and Nicolas Müller refused to show up for work at the town hall. Other local officials followed their lead as did the workers at the Ideal Leather Factory, the chief industry in town. Through leaflets printed and distributed in secret, and by word of mouth, news of the strike spread throughout the country like a wind-whipped brushfire. Mills, factories and mines throughout the country began shutting down with workers refusing to work, even under the threat of death from the appointed German directors of some companies. In Luxembourg City at the central post office, employees busied themselves with the charade of work, moving piles of letters and documents from one bin or pile to the next with no great urgency or purpose. Mail bags were shifted from one end of the room to the other but remained unopened. Piles of packages were left unsorted and undelivered. Throughout the country parents kept their children home from school; teachers who showed up at school simply refused to teach the day's planned lessons; farmers left their cows in the field, no milk would be delivered; laborers simply stayed home; shops and businesses didn't open. In short the country came to an abrupt halt.

Fearing further acts of resistance and protest the German response was swift and lethal. Martial law was declared and striking workers were threatened with immediate execution. Strike organizers including Worré and Müller as well as four of the strike organizers who were teachers from Wiltz were arrested, interrogated, and tried by military tribunal. All were sentenced to death and sent to the Hinzert concentration camp. According to a German officer who witnessed the executions, Worré and Müller cried out "Vive Lëtzebuerg" (Long live Luxembourg) a moment before a spray of bullets ripped into them. The following day the same fate befell the four teachers. One of the strike leaders, Hans Adam a German by birth, had rallied workers in the valley town of Schifflange. He too was arrested but because he was German by birth he was tried as a traitor. Found guilty and sentenced to death he was brought to Cologne where he was publicly beheaded. Family members of all those arrested were rounded up and sent east to prison and labor camps in Germany. In all more than 200 Luxembourgers were arrested with at least 80 of those tried by a special tribunal before being handed over to the Gestapo. Hundreds of prideful high school students who took part in the strike were sent to re-education camps in Germany. The Germans then printed a series of posters bearing the names, occupations and hometowns of those executed and displayed them throughout the country with the intention of shocking the population into submission, and thereby quelling any additional acts of resistance or protest. To Luxembourgers however the posters became symbols of national pride and sovereignty; each a flag of sorts to replace theirs now outlawed.

Liberated since September of 1944 Luxembourg was free and Luxembourg once more. With front line action now well to the east, the country was occupied once again, this time by American troops. Showing few signs of destruction and a people eager to welcome their liberators, Luxembourg proved to be the ideal retreat for battered, war-weary soldiers.

Such was the case in the early afternoon of November 17th, 1944, a day that began with a cold, light rain that would follow the soldiers of the 28th Cavalry Reconnaissance Troop from their defensive positions in the Huertgen Forest to their home for the foreseeable future; the town of Eschweiler.

Suffering from trench-foot, dysentery, illness and some non-battle injuries, the soldiers of the Recon Troop, codenamed "Hotdog", had managed to escape serious battle wounds or worse despite their regular foot and jeep patrols and the constant artillery and mortar attacks during their time in the hell that was the Huertgen. In fact it wasn't until the last night, their last in the forest battle, that a member of their troop was wounded. Soldiers from the 8th Division

Reconnaissance troop began arriving in relief, assuming the various positions throughout the area occupied by the men of the 28th Cavalry Recon Troop. Soldiers of the 28th Recon Troop's first platoon were occupying what was left of German pillboxes that had been captured the previous week. The pillboxes overlooked an unmarked road that ran along the bottom of a steep ravine and that for a short distance paralleled the Kall River. The pillboxes, reachable by a makeshift wooded road that branched from the main road and was congruent with the dense forest, were difficult to locate in daylight let alone during the black of night. When the vehicles of the replacement soldiers began to arrive, the protocol was for occupying soldiers, in this case those from the 28th Recon Troop, to meet the incoming replacements on a marked road and guide them to the well masked pillboxes. That night Corporals Chuck Jones and Loyd Griffin were tasked with guiding two vehicles of the 8th Division Reconnaissance Troop replacements to their location at the pillbox. The pair hiked down the wooded road and met the incoming soldiers' vehicles on a marked section of main road. Jones climbed onto the jeep while Griffin climbed aboard the second vehicle, positioning himself beside the turret of the six-wheeled M-8 light armored scout vehicle, nick-named a "greyhound" by the British troops who also used them. Guided by Jones, the jeep slowly moved forward along the road, the ink black night broken briefly by not too distant flashes of exploding artillery shells reflecting against a low hanging sky. Within a hundred yards of the wooded road to the pillbox outpost a thunderous explosion ripped the night, quaking the road. As if illuminated by a flash of close striking lightning, the road and trees momentarily glowed a brilliant yellow-white, while mud, debris and shrapnel peppered the area. The M-8 Griffin was on had rolled over the mine that the lead jeep had only narrowly missed. The explosion blew the scout car onto its side while pieces of it, blown in every direction, rained onto the road. Griffin and the others in the M-8 were badly wounded, the relatively thin armor flooring of the scout car no match for the blast from the

German mine. Medics from the pillbox and one from the lead jeep rushed in, doing what they could to try to keep Griffin and the others alive until they could be evacuated to an aid station. The medics succeeded.

Now, as the 28th Recon Troop arrived into the sleepy farming community, the rain had all but ceased and a warming sun struggled to emerge from behind retreating clouds desperate to make their stand. Having been reconnoitered prior to their arrival, the town would serve as troop headquarters with soldiers billeted anywhere adequate space could be found. Most of the men would share cramped floor spaces in homes in the village while others would stay in barn lofts or recently deserted homes and buildings, their occupants having chosen to flee before the German occupation or more likely forced out by the Nazis, sometimes in the dead of night; whole families vanishing without a trace. After what they'd lived through for nearly five years, the people in Eschweiler were all too happy to offer whatever they could to the GIs and in turn the soldiers shared what they had with their hosts who, although freed from the Nazi yoke, were left with little to survive on, the Germans having looted anything they considered valuable or possibly useful.

Whenever the troop arrived into a town, it was twenty-four year-old Pvt. George Mergenthaler who was called upon to help facilitate communicating with the townspeople, most of whom would quickly gather to greet the soldiers of the Recon Troop, who in most cases were the first allied soldiers the had ever seen. Fluent in German and French, George was tall, strikingly handsome, and broad-shouldered with soft, sky blue eyes highlighting a matinee idol face that brightened with a wide, engaging, ever present smile. Gracious and charismatic, he spoke with a measured confidence and ease that allowed him to overcome any language obstacles or social apprehensions whenever the Recon Troop had passed through towns and villages in their trek through the war.

Pointing to various houses while reading from a clipboard,

George easily handled introductions, explanations and translations. The entire troop would be spread throughout the village, but the decision was made early on that members of the headquarters platoon would be billeted together or as close as possible for security and ease of communication. To that end George was able to find out after a brief conversation with the town's Mayor and some gathered villagers that the most suitable location for the HQ platoon was in two family farmhouses that were separated by the narrow road that ran through the town. The houses were no more than a few hundred yards from the town church in what could be considered the center of the village and would provide ample space to house all the HQ soldiers. George and fellow headquarters platoon soldiers Cletus La Fond, George Raduykavich, Charles "Stans" Stansbury, Richard Sheesley, Dan Garbo, Lt. Carl Hushes and Capt. Meisenhelter would all take up quarters in the Pletschet family farmhouse, while a few of the other HQ platoon soldiers including Carl Hess and Joe Vocasek were to be billeted across the street in the Huberty home.

Accommodations sorted and men moving, George began gathering his things from the command jeep when one of the men from the town, having remained on the periphery all this time finally approached. Lean and straight backed, the man looked to be in his late thirties with a wave of thick black hair raked back from a soft featured face where deep set eyes sat behind round metal framed glasses. He began speaking to George in forced English but what caught George's attention straight away was the banded white collar peeking through the man's heavy winter coat. Extending a hand he introduced himself as Father Antoine Bodson motioning with a nod over his shoulder at the church sitting at the bend in the road about fifty yards behind George. George responded in German sensing from the priest's patter that it had been quite some time since he'd had the chance to use the classroom English he'd learned somewhere along the way since it appeared he was the only person in town who could speak it at all. On behalf of his flock, Father Bodson welcomed the soldiers to town, noting how happy everyone in town was to have them there, especially after "the way things have been"; no further details given or needed; George understood. On behalf of the troop, while pointing and naming key troop personnel, George thanked the priest and the people of Eschweiler for accommodating the troop, acknowledging the tranquil fields surrounding the town and their striking contrast to where the troop had just been. No further details were given or needed; Father Bodson understood.

In the course of their short but light-hearted conversation it was clear to both men from the beginning, that a quick rapport had been established, as if long lost friends reunited. Eyebrows abruptly arching at the flash of an idea, Father Bodson began stammering through an eager smile, desperately trying to put his thought to word, as if not saying the words fast enough would cause the thought vanish. He had suddenly remembered the spare room in the parsonage that sat a few steps away from where they now stood, opposite the church at the outer bend of another elbow in the road.

"You must...I insist," the priest spoke, nodding and motioning towards the church, doing his best to convince the young soldier.

Surprised and delighted by the offer, George thought for a moment then turned to the Captain and explained the priest's offer. The Captain shrugged his approval noting that the location was still near enough to the rest of the headquarters soldiers should there be a need. It would also mean some extra room for the remaining HQ soldiers billeted in the houses. George made one more query to the priest who assured him that the room was indeed big enough for two soldiers, but only just. George then happily accepted the priest's offer for both he and his best friend in the troop, Cletus La Fond.

George and Cletus followed the priest and took up residence in the small room that had two southward facing windows looking out onto the open pastures and the rolling Luxembourg hills beyond. A small wood burning stove was the only source of heat with candles providing the only light. The two soldiers set up their army issued cots in what would be their home until sometime when the troop was ordered elsewhere.

The rest of the HQ platoon gathered their belongings and made their way to their assigned billets, some grumbling albeit good-naturedly about George and Cletus falling into a pool of luck with their new "private accommodations". As soon as the other soldiers stepped into their assigned houses however their grumbling ceased. A startled silence seized them immediately when they realized their own luck pool. In the Pletschet house lived four sisters between the ages of 17 and 28: Victoria, Anna, Caroline and Claire, while in the Huberty house were three young women, 35-year-old Louise, her 34-year-old sister Léonie-Anne and the youngest sister, 32-year-old Virginia. Over the next several weeks it was no surprise that the Pletschet and Huberty houses saw a near constant flow of foot traffic from Recon Troop soldiers desperately competing for the attention of the girls in each house while the soldiers of "Hotdog" easily assimilated into life in Eschweiler.

When not manning forward observation posts or heading out on infrequent patrols, the soldiers often helped the townspeople with chores on the farms. Conspicuously absent from town were any able-bodied men, now forcibly serving in the Wehrmacht, working in forced labor camps or still in hiding. In their stead the men of the Recon Troop, like George and Cletus, pitched hay, cleaned out barn stalls, chopped wood, fixed fences, carried water, milked cows and otherwise assisted in the various daily tasks of working dairy farms. Perhaps because of an insulated upbringing with no exposure to the workings of field or farm, or perhaps because the daily chores provided a sense of detachment from the horrors of war, George in particular took a keen interest in all there was to do and learn including the milking of the cows, something he'd never done before but quickly developed a skill for. For George, and to a certain degree Cletus, the farm work became therapy, cleansing their thoughts, nurturing their souls and allowing them to return to a simpler life so distant from where they were now. George also found a sense of peace and belonging in the ritual of attending daily mass and receiving communion, his spirit and faith reinvigorated in a time that often seemed devoid of all hope. For George, Eschweiler became a personal oasis.

In the evenings, George and Cletus sometimes took their meals with Father Bodson, his housekeeper and cook endowed with the ability to transform even the most basic ingredients into hearty and flavorful dishes, often with the help of items procured by the soldiers themselves from the company cooks. Since arriving in town, the soldiers were no longer surviving on the cold battlefield K-rations they'd been living on while fighting in the Huertgen. Now company cooks prepared hot meals in a field kitchen set-up in a building situated between the church and the Pletschet house. Often, soldiers were invited to dine with their host families.

In the parsonage, post dinner most nights would find George and Father Bodson listening to music or news on the priest's radio, no longer hidden away from the Nazis, or playing chess or simply sitting and talking for hours, the priest's English improving nightly. It took only a few days before George felt completely at ease in the priest's home, a home that in a way he considered his own. Although thirteen years his elder, George quickly came to think of Father Bodson as an older brother he never had, while the priest was equally taken with George. One evening after dinner, with Cletus having been assigned guard duty for the night, Father Bodson and George sat in the living room of the rectory, by the warming orange glow of a well wooded fire in the stove, and shared family backgrounds.

Antoine Bodson was born in 1907 and was the youngest of 11 children, growing up in Bettange, a small town eight miles south west of Luxembourg city. After his initial schooling in the capital city he answered the calling and entered the seminary at the age of 21. Six years later on the 4th of August 1934, a day after his parents celebrated their 50th wedding anniversary, Father Bodson said his first mass in his hometown. Shortly after that mass he was assigned to a large parish in southern Luxembourg near the French border in the town of Oberkorn where, as an assistant priest, he worked teaching in community with nearly 800 children. When war came to Luxembourg, at the urging of the townspeople, he fled into France but once France surrendered, he returned to Oberkorn. The following year, in November of 1941 he was arrested by the Gestapo and sent to a concentration camp in Germany where for the next five weeks he was interrogated about resistance activities in his parish. Regardless of whether he actually knew anything or not, he told the Gestapo nothing. Upon his release he returned to Oberkorn where he remained until August of 1944 when he was assigned his own parish in the town of Eschweiler and the church of St. Mauritius.

With Father Bodson refilling their glasses, George did his best to satisfy the priest's utter fascination with the state of Texas where George had spent part of his army training. It was a place Father Bodson knew only from the few Hollywood movies he had seen and from books, magazines and newspapers he'd read prior the war. It wasn't George's detailed description of the flat, almost barren landscape or the oppressive, relentless heat, a heat unlike anything George had ever experienced and as one Texan described it, "would fry flies in mid air"; a suffocating heat that rolled across the flatlands on a breeze that brought little relief at best and at worst would hurl dirt and sand at anything in its path, punishing it for daring to be there, stinging exposed flesh such that wasps watched with envy. No, for Father Bodson what seemed almost incomprehensible was the vastness of a land, "just one state" that was so big that within its borders it could swallow the entire country of Luxembourg and most of Europe before running out of room, as George illustrated with a crudely drawn but fairly accurate pencil map of Texas overlaying most of mainland Europe.

With the Calvados adding an extra layer of warmth, George now found it easier to talk beyond the history books and family scrapbooks, while keeping the threatening melancholy at bay. As if in the church confessional, George felt a sudden urge to let loose the burden he'd been carrying with him, the onus he'd felt since he visited London when, for the first time, war's reality struck him and he felt the first stings of German guilt. Like many other soldiers, his name alone billboarded his ancestry to all he met, though it was only George who chose to peel away the veneer exposing what was behind the name. There was no denying his German heritage, one that he'd always been proud of, one that certainly proved useful in his translator role with the Recon Troop and no doubt helped save the lives of his fellow soldiers. With war's end in sight, even though all logic told him there was nothing he could do about the war and all that lead to it, that ancestral pride was now in conflict with the current time and place. He struggled with constant remembrances of the post-war Germany he visited as a youth, the robust cities and the beautiful countryside dotted with storybook towns and magnificent castles all steeped in Teutonic history. The culture and its people, especially his distant relatives, all seemingly so detached from the Germany of today, its cities being reduced to rubble by righteous and vengeful enemies closing in from all sides: its prideful people that George wanted to believe were forced to live, fight and die at the whim of a madman. Father Bodson listened. There was little else he could say or do; no weighted words however well intentioned could assuage George's self imposed guilt. George rose, picking out a piece of wood from the small pile near the stove. He used the tip of his boot to unlatch the door of the hot stove, a maneuver he became adept at the past few evenings, and tossed the wood into the pool of orange embers. With the same boot George pushed the door closed, the thud of iron on iron signaling the end of confession. George sat back down, fingered his glass of Calvados until the silence between them finally reached its limit. He downed a healthy dose of the fiery liquid, swallowed hard and unprompted, began to share with his new brother mile markers along the long road of his family's history, a history that began in Germany, a couple of hundred miles east from where they now sat and only sixteen miles from Stuttgart, in the small river straddling town of Ensingen.

THREE

Ottmar Mergenthaler was the third son of school teacher Johann and his wife Rosina. He entered into the world on May 11th 1854, in the small town of Hachtel, Germany. In autumn of that same year Ottmar's father was transferred to a teaching position in the town of Neuhengstett. Ottmar spent his early childhood there, but at the age of four Johann moved the family again, this time by choice. He was offered and accepted a teaching position in a small town just north of Stuttgart on the Enz River called Ensingen. By this time Rosina had given birth twice more making Ottmar the middle of five children. For a short time the family was happy in their new town, however only a year after the family moved to Ensingen, Rosina died. Ottmar was just five years old. For the next two years Wilhelmine, Rosina's sister, looked after the Mergenthaler children. A loving and caring woman, Wilhelmine tended to the children's needs as if they were her own while Johann continued to support the family at his teaching post. It was also during this time that Johann met and fell in love with the woman who was to become his second wife, Karoline Hahl. In February of 1861 the couple married and by all accounts Karoline easily and happily assumed the role of stepmother to the Mergenthaler children. Because of their father's modest wages the Mergenthaler children had limited opportunities for any formal education, aside from attending their father's primary school. It was during these formative years however that Ottmar began to show signs of a mechanical and technical awareness and curiosity, something that was never more evident than when he was just thirteen years old. At that time the clock in the Ensingen church had been broken for years and despite numerous repair attempts it was declared unfixable by virtually every watch and clock maker in Stuttgart. However Ottmar's fascination with all things mechanical proved overwhelming. For several weeks after school, rather than play with the other children, Ottmar would climb the steps of the church steeple and repeatedly try his young hand at repairing the clock. He was fascinated with the clock's mechanics: the interlacing gears; the weights on rods attached to wound-wire cords threaded through pulleys, the fall for each weight meticulously measured; the precise tension of various coils and springs; the placement and operation of the hammers for the bells. Ottmar became obsessed not necessarily with actually repairing the clock but rather with what he considered to be the brilliance in the clock's design. Examining the various clusters of clock parts on a daily basis honed Ottmar's mechanical reasoning skills and soon the seeming chaotic brush strokes of the clock's inner-workings now painted a vividly detailed painting in Ottmar's mind. Everything made sense; everything came together for a reason, a reason that to Ottmar was clear and logical. One evening as the sun began to set and evensong approached, the church bells suddenly rang out.

"The schoolmaster's son has done it", stunned townspeople shouted as a grinning Ottmar emerged from the church. From then on in Ensingen, Ottmar was known as the "whiz kid". Fixing the church clock also cemented Ottmar's desire to become a watchmaker. Although his father had hoped and tried to convince Ottmar to follow in his footsteps and become a school teacher, he eventually relented and the following year fourteen-year-old Ottmar left school for a four-year apprenticeship as a watchmaker with his stepmother's brother in Bietigheim, Germany.

Ottmar moved in with his step-uncle Louis Hahl and was immediately accepted into the family. In accordance with the terms of the apprenticeship, Ottmar was to provide his own tools and would work for four years without pay. In return, he received room and board and most importantly experience. He worked long hours, honing his technical skills and satisfying his thirst for mechanical knowledge. It was during this time that Ottmar's quick comprehension and proficiency matured. He came to accept the beauty in precision crafting, developing an uncanny ability to view the mechanics of any mechanism as whole rather than a collection of parts. Viewing mechanics in such a way allowed Ottmar's technical skills to rapidly advance and it wasn't long before he was drafting technical drawings and preparing patent applications. For Ottmar, the four year apprenticeship passed quickly, and it became clear to all that he had outgrown the challenges at his step-uncle's shop and began to look elsewhere to further his ambitions. In the steady and rapidly growing industries and technologies of the time, Ottmar saw greater potential for his unique skills, and the best chance to apply those skills, across the Atlantic.

In 1872 with the help of his step-uncle, eighteen year old Ottmar Mergenthaler boarded the steamship *SS Berlin* and headed to his future in America. Louis Hahl's son August had emigrated to the United States years earlier and was in charge of an electronics and patent model development workshop in Washington, DC, coincidently the home of the US Patent Office, a mecca for anyone with design, engineering and invention ambitions. At his father's urging, August Hahl offered young Mergenthaler a position and advanced him the money necessary to secure passage. Much like his apprenticeship for the elder Hahl, Ottmar was to work for his step-cousin while working off his debt. On October 26, 1872, with only $30 in his pocket and speaking no English, the fit and handsome, blue-eyed, reddish-blond haired Mergenthaler stepped onto the teeming docks in Baltimore. As planned he then travelled by train to Washington where he would begin working at the shop, paying off his debt and soaking up any and all experiences.

He had no previous knowledge or experience working in electrical instrument manufacturing, but Mergenthaler was able to learn quickly and soon took a leading role in the workshop as a manager and foreman. A year after his arrival the economy turned and the business was forced to move to Baltimore, at that time a major industrial hub that also sported a large German-American population. While most of the workers at the shop had to be laid-off because of the flagging economy, August kept his step-cousin on, well aware of Mergenthaler's keen sense of mechanical and technical design drafting skills. The move turned out to be fortuitous for both Hahl and Mergenthaler. Surrounded by German-Americans, Mergenthaler wasted no time socializing and integrating into American society and culture while devoting himself to learning English until he could speak it fluently, albeit with a thick, guttural accent. Outside of work, Mergenthaler kept company with other young Germans who lived together, sang together, dined together and often took long walks together and it was in this close circle of friends that the usually introverted Ottmar would come alive.

Not long after the company's move to Baltimore, a stranger walked into Hahl's workshop, having heard about a young German immigrant working there who possessed remarkable mechanical and technical engineering insight. Charles T. Moore brought with him a patented, self-designed typewriting machine. His idea was to use this machine to eliminate hand-set type currently used in the newspaper business. However Moore's invention was unreliable at best and simply did not operate as he had intended. After a brief examination of the machine, Mergenthaler realized that the problem was not with the mechanics and assemblage but rather with Moore's initial machine design. Knowing he was out of his design depth, Moore commissioned Mergenthaler to try and improve the machine, and although Mergenthaler did eventually improve on the typewriter's overall functionality as he had been commissioned to do, it would never work well enough for mass use in the newspaper industry. What the machine did very well however was put flame to Mergenthaler's burning interest in the mechanical print process. This in turn attracted the attention of Charles Moore's sponsors and financiers.

In 1877, a year after Moore first brought his machine to Mergenthaler, those financiers founded the National Machine Printing Company for the sole purpose of bankrolling other inventions aimed at advancing the long established printing techniques of the time, especially with regard to newspapers, the main conveyance of news and information. Publishers sought ways to dramatically improve the speed and efficiency of publishing and distributing mass quantities of newspapers however the main problem was improving the slow, cumbersome typesetting process.

The National Machine Printing Company immediately commissioned Mergenthaler to build a machine based on the design of one of the investors, James Clephane. The basic idea of Celphane's machine called for molten metal to be poured into papier-mâché molds of individual text characters. Those characters would then be arranged to create lines of text or matrices for plate printing. While the idea was sound, the process was laborious and therefore time consuming. Much like Moore's typewriter, Mergenthaler immediately noticed the faulty machine design plans but Clephane brushed aside Mergenthaler's objections and the build process continued. A year later Mergenthaler presented the completed machine as specified, and like Moore's typewriter it never functioned well enough or reliably enough for widespread continuous use. However as Mergenthaler built Clephane's machine he saw elements in it that had potential and he was now consumed by a passion to improve and build upon Clephane's design. While working on building Clephane's machine he simultaneously began developing his own print machine models.

By 1881 Mergenthaler's personal and professional lives were flourishing. Due partly to his exhaustive dedication, drive, passion and ambition and his growing reputation, he and Hahl now entered into a partnership in the business. Despite working tirelessly, Mergenthaler also found time to step outside of the shop and enjoy all his new found home in America had to offer. He was charismatic, jovial, gregarious and generous. A member of the Zion church of Baltimore, Mergenthaler also joined German social groups and societies where he enjoyed drinking and dining with friends, smoking his pipe and cigars and joking and singing. It was said that he had a rich baritone voice and even joined the Liederkranz singing club of Baltimore and would eventually become its president. It was there too that he met and fell in love with Emma Lachenmayer and in September of that year they married. Two years later the couple had their first child, a boy, Fritz Lilian. That same year Mergenthaler decided he'd outgrown Hahl's workshop and struck out on his own. Free to choose his own projects, Mergenthaler had an idea for a new machine that would utilize line-by-line matrices versus individual letter stamping in the papier-mâché strips, thus speeding up typesetting and the overall printing process. He approached James Clephane with whom by now he had developed a deep friendship. Intrigued by the design, Clephane presented the plans to his partners and by late 1883 Mergenthaler was put in charge of the workshop of the newly formed National Typographic Company. There he worked feverishly on his invention and by year's end he produced a small prototype that was known as the "band machine" because of the narrow brass bands, each of which contained the entire alphabet, hanging side-by-side in the machine and related to a specific key on a keyboard. When an operator typed, these bands were brought into alignment forming words and justified with spacers between words. The line of text was then cast into the paper-mache molds using molten metal producing a slug of text ready for printing. Although the machine functioned as expected several problems were immediately evident not the least of which was the slow drying time of the matrices that would in turn greatly reduce printing speed and efficiency, and the inability to correct typing mistakes. Still Mergenthaler's prototype band machine demonstrated that a better, more efficient method of typesetting and mass printing, something virtually unchanged since Gutenberg's printing press, was possible. The band machine also convinced his financiers that unlike other would-be inventors of the time, Mergenthaler was onto something and they continued to bankroll his endeavors.

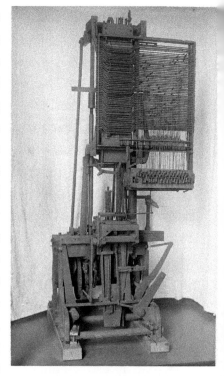

Mergenthaler's Band Machine
photo: National Archives

Always the perfectionist and optimist, Mergenthaler once again returned to his drafting table applying his technical ingenuity and first-hand knowledge of precision crafting in the pursuit of designing and building the perfect printing machine. Mergenthaler toiled tirelessly believing that if he worked through the design and engineering flaws of the band machine a better more reliable machine was possible. He worked exhaustive hours often on his own, long after his employees had left for the day, usually losing track of time and working late into the night. He became obsessed with the idea of building the perfect printing machine. Still Mergenthaler never lost sight of that which was most important to him: his family, and he was committed to spending every available bit of free time with his wife Emma and now children, having welcomed his second son Julius into the world in 1884.

Later that same year while riding a train to Washington for a meeting with Clephane and Lemon Hine the majority shareholding in the National Typographic Company, Mergenthaler stared distractedly out the window, a proud father once again. Thinking of his newest son allowed his mind to wander to the days of his own youth in Germany and studying at his father's school. There books were expensive and scarce. Mergenthaler hoped that someday his inventions would allow for the inexpensive production of books and reading materials, making them available to anyone. Blurs of buildings passed while fragmented images of his early life vied for his attention; a memory of the school teacher father who he hadn't seen in years. What would his father think of his son now, a son who had turned his back on his father's profession to pursue his own path, only now to be working on an invention that would ultimately benefit his father, other teachers and pupils the world over? There were haunting scenes too, flashes of the mother he barely knew and of the aunt who helped raise him. He remembered his stepmother Karoline and the day she married his father, the family once again whole and happy.

"Springerle." Mergenthaler's back straightened, his head lifted, his eyes darted. His mouth and lips formed the word that only he heard: "Springerle". His mind raced; memories swirled. "Springerle": traditional German holiday cookies or biscuits, their tops often embossed with ornate designs. Made by pressing a mold or an embossed rolling pin onto the dough and allowing the impression to dry preserved the detail of the surface pattern during baking. It was these traditional holiday treats or more exactly how they were made that flashed through Ottmar's mind. He stared intently out the window, looking well beyond the passing towns and landscapes, seeing none. The memories came in a torrent, suddenly remembering helping his stepmother make the holiday treats, and that one year when he presented his stepmother with the hand-carved "Springerle" mold he'd spent weeks crafting. The torrent ebbed leaving a pool of memories, ideas, and dreams from which sprang the answer that had eluded Mergenthaler until that very moment. To the rhythmic thump and clatter of the speeding train, Mergenthaler realized that the future of mass printing lay not in separate machines for casting and stamping, but in a single machine that could do both. With the memories of youth fresh and clear, Mergenthaler now knew exactly how to go about it. In a rush the detailed mechanism blueprinted in his mind; the assemblage of parts that would trigger the embossing of letters into thin, pliable brass strips using the stroke of a key from a keyboard. The embossed matrices would then serve as the casting molds and as Mergenthaler now envisioned, it could all be done on the same machine. "Springerle."

His goal within sight, his thoughts and actions engulfed by a merciless passion and burning determination, Mergenthaler poured himself into his work leaving room for little else. Now however his ambition was spurred by the support and backing from some of the biggest names in the newspaper business. After several patented attempts, it was in the summer of 1885 that Mergenthaler had finally built the machine that would revolutionize printing. "The Blower" as it was known because it operated with the use of compressed air, was first commercially demonstrated in the composing room of the *New York Tribune* newspaper. Among those in attendance was the paper's publisher Whitelaw Reid. With a small crowd looking on, Mergenthaler sat at the keyboard of his new invention and began typing. The machine hissed and whirred, metal pieces slid along tracks, then a thin metal strip bearing the words Mergenthaler typed slid down into a tray. Onlookers were amazed and it was when Reid exclaimed, "Ottmar you've done it! It's a line of type" that Mergenthaler's "Linotype" machine was christened. That same year the Mergenthalers also christened their third son Eugene.

Over the next year as Mergenthaler worked at perfecting the machine, the Mergenthaler Printing Company was founded with the financial backing of the newspaper industry icons of the time. Prior to Mergenthaler's invention no newspaper in the world was more than eight pages in total and in this new age of rapidly expanding industry and communication Mergenthaler's invention arrived at the perfect time. His new company was now tasked with the mass production of the Linotype machine. One hundred new machines were ordered by his newspaper backers and on July 3, 1886 the first of the initial twelve ordered by Whitelaw Reid's *New York Tribune* was put into action. The *New York Tribune* became the first newspaper to use the Linotype on a daily basis. As production of the Linotype machines ramped-up, the ever driven Mergenthaler continually looked for ways of perfecting his invention. Between the time the New York Tribune received its first machine and delivery of the last of the dozen ordered, Mergenthaler had filed another nine patented improvements.

A year later in 1887 Herman Charles Mergenthaler, Ottmar and Emma's fourth son, was born. By that time another hundred Linotype machines were on order and even as Mergenthaler continued to make improvements to his invention, demand was now outpacing supply. He was forced to expand his workshop in Baltimore and quadrupled the workforce, while opening another factory nearby with more than a hundred employees working on machine assembly and matrix production. Larger parts production was farmed out to factories elsewhere in Baltimore and New York. By the time the year drew to a close, the *New York Tribune* had thirty Linotype machines, the *Washington Post* half as many while newspapers in Chicago and Louisville had twenty and eighteen machines respectively. Also published that same year was the first book printed entirely by using the Linotype, *The Tribune Book of Open Air Sports* with a note on the verso of the title page that read: "This book is printed without type, being the first product in book form of the Mergenthaler machine which wholly supersedes the use of movable type."

Mergenthaler's business growth, spurred by considerable financial backing, allowed him personal prosperity as well. He moved the family to a large house in an upscale area of Baltimore where his insistence that the close-knit family spend plenty of time together included horse riding every evening after dinner and bringing the

Ottmar Mergenthaler
Photo: Mergenthaler Family Collection

entire family on business trips whenever possible. However Mergenthaler's triumphs as an inventor and his success in business were to be challenged with misfortune in his personal life. In early 1888 at the age of four, Ottmar's son Julius died suddenly. Julius' death devastated Ottmar and had a profound and lasting impact on Mergenthaler who now threw himself into his work as a means of coping with his grief. Unfortunately this would not be the last time the Mergenthaler family would encounter tragedy. By autumn of that same year the combined emotional, physical and business pressures may have contributed to Mergenthaler's near fatal bout of pleurisy, a condition where the membrane lining the chest cavity and the layer of tissue that surrounds the lungs becomes inflamed causing sharp, crippling chest pains. Mergenthaler struggled through every pressured breath and the severe burning sensation that seized his chest. It would take months for Mergenthaler to recover but not before strengthening his commitment to family, both his immediate family and the family back in Germany whom he was now helping financially.

Healthy and reinvigorated by an unquenched drive for self-defined measures of success and perfection, Mergenthaler continued to build upon his earlier achievements even as his factories, now retooled and staffed for assembly line machine production, desperately worked to fulfill orders. In early 1890 Mergenthaler introduced his new "Square Based" machine, a comparatively smaller and more efficient model that could be made less expensively without sacrificing efficiency. By all accounts Mergenthaler's newest model was hailed as an unparalleled success. Mergenthaler however remained unsatisfied. Even as the newest models rolled off the line, he pressed forward with changes both subtle and significant, streamlining his invention in his quest for perfection. In September of that same year he would file a patent for a new model, the Linotype "Simplex" machine. This would prove to be Mergenthaler's greatest technical achievement; a machine so advanced that Thomas Edison would praise it as being the Eighth Wonder of the World. Ahead of its time, it was the Simplex machine that any and all improvements going forward would be based upon; a model so well designed and precision tooled that it would remain virtually unchanged for the next hundred years.

While the Linotype machine was gaining in popularity by newspapers that could afford it in America, Mergenthaler's machines were also garnering international attention with patent rights having been sold to Great Britain and Ireland for $2.5 million.

Stubborn, lacking in boardroom diplomacy yet beloved by his employees, Mergenthaler often clashed with business partners and investors. That, matched with the overwhelming demand for his invention, would eventually lead to Mergenthaler establishing his own stand-alone company in 1891: the Mergenthaler Linotype Company, headquartered in Brooklyn, NY. It would be the first time the word "Linotype" was included in a company name.

Now at the height of his professional achievements it was in early 1894 that his wife gave birth to the couple's only daughter, Pauline who, according to Mergenthaler, "provided the missing piece of a well-composed family." However the joy Pauline brought to the Mergenthaler family would be countered later that year when Ottmar would once again be confronted with health problems. His insatiable drive and ambition, long hours and the stresses of a rapidly growing business over the last dozen years had finally taken their physical toll. Mergenthaler was diagnosed with tuberculosis.

The Mergenthaler family on vacation (L-R) Herman, Fritz, Ottmar, Emma, Pauline (in the arms of her nanny), and Eugene

Photo: Mergenthaler Family Collection

For the next few years as the business bearing his name thrived, Mergenthaler would move the family several times in an effort to find treatment and comfort for his ill health. He first sought relief in the Blue Mountains in Maryland but finding little improvement for his condition, moved to Saranac Lake in the Adirondacks of upstate New York. His stay there would be short lived as the cold weather proved to be too taxing to his system. In late 1895 he moved the family to the American southwest, first to Prescott, Arizona and then a year later settling in to Deming, New Mexico where he took the time to pen his memoirs. Two years later misfortune would find Mergenthaler once again when a fire razed his New Mexico home. Although no one from the family was injured, the fire destroyed everything including his newly completed autobiography. His health deteriorating rapidly, the family was forced to move once again, this time returning to their Baltimore home in mid-April, 1897. Two years later on October 28, 1899 Ottmar Mergenthaler died in his home surrounded by his family. He was 45 years old.

After his death, Mergenthaler's company kept pace with advancing technologies, continuing to grow and thrive until the industry saw the arrival of phototypesetting and computerization, something Mergenthaler alluded to nearly a century earlier. It was in February of 1885 at an exhibition of his "band machine" and a banquet in his honor at the Chamberlain Hotel in Washington D.C., in front of a gathering of invited guests including President Chester Arthur, senators and congressmen and leading newspaper publishers of the time, that Mergenthaler remarked, "I am convinced, gentlemen, that unless some method of printing can be designed which requires no type at all, the method embodied in our invention will be the one used in the future."

In accordance with his will, Ottmar Mergenthaler's estate was divided amongst his family with his wife Emma receiving a third of his wealth while the other two-thirds of his fortune would go to his children who would be eligible to collect their inheritance on their twenty-first birthdays. Mergenthaler's total fortune at that time, including stocks and bonds, calculated in today's dollars, was estimated at more than $43-million.

The Mergenthaler Company remained in existence for nearly a hundred years before being acquired by a German firm in 1987.

FOUR

Family wealth and Ottmar's insistence allowed his children to receive the highest quality education. While all three sons would attend Cornell University, Pauline attended Notre Dame College in Govanstown, Maryland and would marry in 1917 at the age of 23, giving birth to a daughter, Nancy, a year later. The few family members close to her said she was a woman well ahead of her time, a free thinking spirit who never minced words nor shied away from speaking her mind on the wealth of far ranging topics of the time. She could at different times and in equal measures be hard and unaffectionate, then welcoming and gregarious. Unfortunately her marriage began to deteriorate not long after Nancy was born, and in 1925 Pauline was granted a full divorce on the grounds of abandonment. She never remarried and at the time of her death in 1986, at the age of 91, was living in an elder care home in Washington, D.C. By this time daughter Nancy had also settled in the Washington area to look after her aging mother. Nancy never married and died in 1996.

Ottmar's eldest son Fritz studied mechanical engineering at Cornell, graduating in 1905. Shortly after, he began working as a vice president at the Mergenthaler Company, although he quickly developed interests in other business ventures such as investing in profitable gold mines in New Mexico as well as real estate development. One of those real estate investments was in the Cape May Real Estate Company where Fritz became a stockholder. The Company was headed by prominent Baltimore attorney Frederick Feldner, whose shrewd business sense and political connections translated into a proven record of successful real estate deals, business investments and government contracts. As director of the Maryland Dredging Company, Feldner secured a million dollar government project for dredging Baltimore's harbor as well as a lucrative contract for draining the Florida Everglades for future development. Feldner was also president of the Colombia United States Mining Company, a position that no doubt aided in his being appointed consul for the Republic of Colombia in Baltimore.

Greatly admiring his business acumen, Fritz's association with Feldner ran beyond the business realm. It was in the social climate and circles of the time that Fritz met Feldner's daughter Doris. Wildly popular amongst her set, young and petite with long flowing brown hair, an engaging wide smile and beguiling eyes, Doris was often demure and vivacious in equal measures. Men always wanted to talk to her or be seen talking to her; women talked about her. It was said that the success of any must-attend social event of the time was often gauged by her presence. It was at one of those gatherings that she met Fritz Mergenthaler and the two quickly fell in love. It wasn't long before newspaper society columns announced the couple's engagement.

Around the time of the engagement Fritz's next youngest brother Eugene Mergenthaler, who like his older brother was also studying mechanical engineering at Cornell, chose to leave the upstate NY campus and study abroad at one of the top engineering schools, the Karlsruhe Institute of Technology in Germany. Although his initial reason for the move was to broaden his educational experience, he also had a yearning to know more about his ancestral homeland, to reconnect with his relatives and to break the pattern of all three Mergenthaler boys attending the same university, as by this time his younger brother Herman, having completed studies at the private Lawrenceville School, was now set to attend Cornell in pursuit of a law degree.

While in Germany, Eugene quickly renewed relationships with his cousins. As a young boy he and the rest of the family would often accompany his father on business trips or on trips home when Ottmar would visit his father or siblings. Speaking fluent German, he was able to assimilate into the German culture easily. However in late May of 1907 trouble would mar his stay. While driving through the German countryside with two classmates, Eugene at the wheel and driving much too fast on the unpaved and wildly winding roads, encountered a sudden sharp curve and lost control. The car careened off the road, crashing headlong into a ditch. Eugene was unhurt, however one of the classmates riding with him was thrown from the car and severely injured. After investigating the accident, German police arrested Eugene. He was held on a $25,000 bond, an enormous sum at the time, due to what police considered to be dangerous and reckless driving and the severity of the injuries resulting from the crash. Authorities also considered him a flight risk since he was a student carrying an American passport and had the wealth and connections to leave the country immediately if he so desired.

Eugene was allowed to contact his family and knowing that the Mergenthaler name would certainly draw attention, sent a cryptic cable to his mother stating only the most basic facts and circumstances. Still, newspapers picked up the story and ran with what little they had, stating only the most basic facts of the accident and that he'd been arrested. A little more than a week after receiving the cable, Fritz boarded a steam ship bound for Europe, where he was to pay the bond and according to one newspaper account, "represent the family in Eugene's interest". Paying cash, Fritz secured Eugene's release while also assuring authorities that the Mergenthaler family would cover all medical costs and pay for any damages or miscellaneous expenses resulting from the accident. Eugene was never formally charged and returned to America with his brother. Once back on his native soil, Eugene left Cornell University, finishing his degree at John Hopkins University. Upon graduation, like his brother before him, he too immediately went to work at the Mergenthaler Linotype Company, assuming a role as a vice president.

While Eugene was just beginning his tenure in the family business, Fritz was becoming less involved in the Mergenthaler Linotype Company, thanks to a deepening mentor relationship with Frederick Feldner and his love interest in Doris. In what was the social event of the summer of 1909, with Eugene serving as best man, Fritz and Doris were married under an enormous white tent on the front lawn of the Feldner's country summer home on the ninth of June. The very next day the couple boarded the steamship *SS La Provence** leaving New York bound for Le Harve for a honeymoon trip that would have them traveling throughout Europe by car, stopping at nearly every major European city. For the tall, dashing fair-haired Fritz and his enchanting bride Doris the future looked bright. They were young, in love, wealthy and looking to start their own family. The whole of their lives was set to unfold.

That following year, 1910, would prove pivotal for the Mergenthaler family. Eugene grew restless working for Mergenthaler Linotype Company, weary of the relentless and near suffocating reminders of a company built upon his father's inventiveness, tireless work and dedication. With his brother Fritz no longer involved in the

---

* *The SS La Provence would be taken over by the French government during WWI and renamed the SS Provence II, an armed merchant cruiser that was converted to a troop transport ship. On February 26, 1916, while operating in the Mediterranean Sea, the SS Provence II was torpedoed by German submarine U-35, commanded by Lothar von Arnauld de la Periere who would become the most successful U-boat captain of all time. The SS Provence II sank, killing 930 people.*

Fritz and Doris, May 1910
Photo: Mergenthaler Family Collection

day-to-day operations, it was Eugene who bore the burden of maintaining the Mergenthaler family presence in the company. Paired with the self-imposed encumbrance of having to live up to his father's accomplishments, Eugene was overcome by a need to step out from under Ottmar's ever lingering shadow to make his own mark in the business world. To achieve that goal Eugene established his own mechanical design company in Baltimore: The Eugene Mergenthaler Company. Here Eugene had the freedom to work on and cultivate projects suited to his liking while applying intricate mechanical design skills that would have made his father proud. In February of that year his company filed a patent for the first of its many inventions: a safety razor. Although safety razors had existed for some time, Eugene's innovative design called for a thin strip of coiled, razor-edged material to be spooled along a narrow guide, thereby exposing the cutting edge. As the blade became dull the user could simply loosen the handle, advance the strip to a fresh-edged portion and then retighten the handle, locking the strip blade in place. While his safety razor was ingenious in design, it proved to be commercially impractical, especially in light of the Gillette Company's eventual mass market acceptance of their new disposable blade razor introduced later that same year. While both products struggled to gain footing initially, it would be years later in 1914, at the start of World War One, when the Gillette Company would secure a government contract to supply razors to troops overseas. That combined with relentless advertising and marketing would cement the Gillette Company's market dominance. Still believing in his innovation, Eugene would continue to look for ways of improving his design to challenge Gillette's hold on the safety razor market but ultimately his efforts would prove fruitless and he would eventually abandon his concept, relegating it to an historical reference page in a dusty tome of the patent office.

A few months after Eugene filed his safety razor patent, the Mergenthaler family would celebrate another wedding. On April 12, 1910, youngest son Herman, while attending Cornell on the Ithaca, NY campus, met Alice Sweeney whose family was from nearby Rochester. Her father George Sweeney was the proprietor of the Rochester Hotel, and would later go on to be vice president and general manager of the Commodore Hotel* in New York City, at that time one of the top luxury hotels in Manhattan, adjacent to Grand Central Terminal. Herman and Alice announced their engagement at the beginning of March and set the wedding date for a month later. The ceremony took place at the Victoria Hotel, where at that time Alice's father was the general manager. Once again Eugene would serve as best man ,while Herman's sister Pauline was chosen as the maid of honor. Like Fritz and Doris had done the year before, newlyweds Herman and Alice traveled throughout Europe by car for the rest of the spring and into

---

* *Named after "Commodore" Cornelius Vanderbilt, the founder of New York Central Railroad, the hotel opened on January 28, 1919 boasting the "Most Beautiful Lobby in The World," complete with a waterfall. Successful for more than half a century, the hotel began losing money in the late 1970s when its parent company, the Penn Central Railroad went into bankruptcy. Bought and remodeled by the Trump Organization in partnership with the Hyatt Corporation the hotel re-opened in 1980 as the Grand Hyatt New York.*

early summer. The joyful celebration of Herman and Alice's marriage would grace the society pages and mark a high point for the Mergenthaler family that year, a high point that was to be short lived.

Herman's oldest brother Fritz, married the year before, had all but completely stepped away from the company that bore his family name and out from the comforting shadow of his father's legacy. He began investing in various emerging companies and was

Alice Sweeney on her wedding day
Photo: Mergenthaler Family Collection

determined to learn what he could from his father-in-law while trying his hand in real estate development. In early August Fritz and Doris along with her parents traveled to Atlantic City for a weekend away from the sweltering summer city heat of Baltimore. They spent the days wading in the cool waters of the Atlantic, riding horses along the beach or strolling along the famous boardwalk with other tourists as the setting sun painted the ocean peaks a vibrant orange and the cool briny breeze soothed. It was time well spent away from a city's demanding grind.

The weekend over, the party set out late in the afternoon on Tuesday, August 9 in Feldner's recently purchased Lozier Touring Car driven by his chauffeur Milton Jones. They were heading for Cape May where Doris and her mother Amalia would relax on the shaded hotel veranda overlooking the ocean while reading, chatting, playing cards and sipping cocktails. If it wasn't too oppressively humid, they might consider wandering along the boardwalk that weaved along the oceanfront on the edge of the still developing town. Later they'd walk along the magnificent expanse of beach fronting the hotel watching the late day Atlantic waves roll in, letting the cool water lap at their bare feet.

Meantime Fritz and Frederick planned to check the progress of the latest and on-going Cape May Real Estate Company project: the development of Cape May intended to rival the upscale coastal resort towns such as Newport, Rhode Island and the Hamptons on Long Island while attracting society's wealthy and elite. Already a popular vacation destination, the development of "East Cape May Project" began in 1904, with plans that called for dredging Cape May Harbor then using the excavated earth to help fill in four-square miles of land that would eventually be studded with lavish mansions, a nearby yacht club, a championship golf course, a town center, an airport and above all, the Hotel Cape May.

Hotel Cape May, 1913
photo: National Archives

A masterpiece of Beaux-arts style, the two-story lobby was pillared by the finest Italian marble columns, appointed with gleaming ornate fixtures and luxuriously furnished with the finest materials and pieces of the time. Guests walked upon an intricately designed hand-laid mosaic floor while a magnificent stained glass dome arched overhead bathing the lobby in a warm rich glowing light. Every detail of the hotel emoted opulence with no cost spared in construction or decor. Eight stories tall with 333 rooms, the Hotel Cape May* had a cavernous grand ballroom, a 350-seat Corinthian columned dining room, a swimming pool, a bowling alley, a gymnasium and sweeping views of the Atlantic Ocean. Two years behind schedule and costing more than one-million dollars (more than double the intended budget) the hotel finally opened with great fanfare in April of 1908 and was the largest hotel in the world at the time. Almost immediately afterwards however, mechanical, design and operational problems forced it to close for repairs only six months later. Continued repair setbacks and supply delays as well as labor issues proved financially overwhelming, forcing the company to declare bankruptcy. Seeing an opportunity, Feldner swooped in to become the company's new president and major stockholder. Under his stewardship and with Fritz by his side, the East Cape May project was once again moving forward.

Planning to meet friends for an early dinner followed by cocktails on the hotel's veranda while moonlit waves broke along the shore, their car sped along the newly completed state road, the one that afforded greater and more direct access to Cape May from Atlantic City. Somewhere along the road Fritz, wanting to arrive at the hotel behind the wheel of his new, expensive car, decided to drive the rest of the way, with Jones moving to the front passenger seat. One by one

---

* *During its life the hotel passed between several owners, survived numerous bankruptcies, was used as a military hospital during WWI and WWII, was later renamed the Admiral Hotel and then the Christian Admiral Hotel. After falling into disrepair when its last owner went bankrupt and no buyer could be found to save it, the hotel was demolished in 1996 to make way for beachfront townhouses.*

Fritz overtook other drivers along the road as they approached the Mill Lane railroad crossing a few miles north of their destination and a few minutes before six o'clock. Here the road narrowed and was walled along the left side with the tall, frayed, wind whipped stalks of summer cornfields.

Living near the crossing, May MacNeill was sitting on her front porch enjoying the cool evening sea breeze as the day's scorching sun slid slowly down a hazy summer sky. She saw everything clearly. Springing from her chair she vaulted down the three wooden porch steps and rushed towards the road. It became clear that she wouldn't reach the road in time and began waving wildly while yelling at the approaching car. The engine roared when the long, sleek Lozier sped past, leaving a cloud of road dust in its wake. Whether the tightly clustered rows of corn stalks obscured Fritz's view on the left, or he didn't see the waving woman approaching the roadside from the right, or he simply chose to ignore her, or he felt they could make, it will never be known.

Engineer Joseph Wheaton saw the car barreling up the road. He desperately but futilely tried to cut the power while blasting the piercing whistle of The Cape May Express train four times, the last coming just moments before the car's front wheels cleared the first set of iron rails and crested the tracks. An instant later the hurtling train slammed into the car squarely between the front and rear wheels, launching it into the air, obliterating it on impact and instantly killing everyone inside. Such was the force of the collision that it broke the locomotive's piston and ripped the cast iron steps of the cab completely from the train. What was left of the car rolled several times, tossing clothing, personal items, jewelry and body parts along the tracks for more than two hundred feet. The blood soaked bodies of the Feldners and Mergenthalers were found nearly two dozen yards from the site of impact, while pieces of the car were found more than a hundred yards away.

The first to arrive on the grisly scene found Frederick Feldner's body first. His head had been smashed in on one side and his entire chest cavity was missing from his disemboweled body. Mrs. Feldner's head was crushed into a mass of unrecognizable blood and tissue while the body of their beautiful daughter Doris was torn and mangled beyond recognition, identified only by process of elimination. Fritz's body was horribly mutilated from being dragged partway down the tracks by the train; his head nearly severed. Chauffeur Jones' body was discovered crushed into what was left of the car, now a blood soaked mound of twisted metal, leather and wood. As it pulled into the Cape May station much later than scheduled that Tuesday evening, most passengers waiting on the station platform failed to notice the bits of flesh stuck onto the train's blood covered wheels.

Married just fourteen months, twenty-seven year old Fritz Mergenthaler and his twenty-two year old wife Doris were buried together three days later in the Mergenthaler family plot in Loudon Park cemetery in Baltimore.

The tragic accident devastated the Mergenthaler family, yet drew them closer together. Eugene, who had been living in Germany and had come back when he received the shocking news of his brother's death, decided to return to the US to care for his grieving mother and to assume the stabilizing role his older brother had played in helping to raise Pauline, now a precocious, headstrong sixteen year old. Both brothers however sought relief from their grief by focusing on the more mundane and pragmatic matters of business.

Herman, recently graduated, dove into the family business as a secretary focusing on the day-to-day operations while learning the intricacies and politics involved in running the Mergenthaler Linotype Company. Herman also saw through to completion a land acquisition deal his brother Fritz had started as one of his first real estate projects. For a brief time Herman was president of Llenroc Farms in Broad Brook, New Jersey, the farm's name a tribute to the school the brothers attended in happier times: "Cornell" spelled backwards. Eugene, in need of Herman's legal guidance and business acumen, invited

Herman to join the company as a vice president in the growing business.

Eugene meantime concentrated on enhancing and building upon the design of his safety razor and in 1912 he patented his next invention based on his previous work. If Eugene's razor was to find success, he reasoned, a means of sharpening and reusing the thin strip razor tape was necessary. His latest device was to be the solution and Eugene, now more determined than ever to see his invention a success, continued marketing his design, however two years later the outbreak of war would put an end his efforts.

In 1914 the "war to end all wars" erupted in Europe. It would eventually involve most of the European nations as well as Russia, Middle Eastern countries and in 1917, the United States. In February of 1917, the United States broke off relations with Germany, and the need to bolster military strength ahead of entry into the war led to enacting the Selective Service Act in May of that year. All males between the ages of eighteen and thirty-one were to register for conscription into service. Herman, now thirty years old, registered for the draft on June 5th of that year but would not get called to service until April the following year, two days after his thirty-first birthday. Although fluent in German, Herman was stationed stateside at the headquarters for the 3rd Navy District in Brooklyn, New York, a short distance from his Park Avenue home. He began his service as a machinist's mate second class, but four months later was promoted to first class and by the time the war ended Herman was honorably discharged as a Chief Machinist's Mate.

Although two years beyond the age for required registration, and with Pauline now married, Eugene insisted on doing his part for the war effort. On September 12th, 1918 he registered for service at his local draft board in Baltimore. Nearly two months to the day after he was officially registered, the war ended on November 11, 1918, without Eugene being called to arms. The world celebrated the end of a four-year long war that ultimately claimed the lives of more than 8.5-

million soldiers. Civilian death totals were even higher at more than 13 million, although some of those killed no doubt fell victim to the Spanish Flu epidemic that was only in the nascent stages at the war's end. With no effective antibiotics or vaccines available to treat this flu strain or prevent the spread, it would grow to become the deadliest flu pandemic the world would ever see. In little more than a year, an estimated 500-million people were stricken with the flu with between 30-50 million people, nearly one-fifth of the world's total population, dying from it. In the United States more than a quarter of the country's entire population became infected, resulting in more than 675,000 deaths. Most of the flu's victims were young and healthy adults between the ages of 20 and 40 with many dying from pneumonia when the flu virus aggressively attacked their respiratory systems. Eugene Mergenthaler was one of those victims.

Christmas 1918 in the Mergenthaler family was setting up to be unlike any holiday the family had experienced in quite some time. Pauline had given birth to Nancy earlier in the year and the idea of the family being together for her first Christmas excited all. On Christmas day they gathered at the Mergenthaler family home in Baltimore. There was plenty of good cheer to go around, however as evening drew near, Eugene began feeling fatigued and achy, his limbs sometimes seemed heavy and at times he felt a rush of warmth wash over his neck and shoulders. A nagging cough began to develop. At first he and others thought nothing of it, believing he'd simply caught a common cold, his mother, as mothers do, reminding him to drink plenty of fluids to flush the cold from his system and get plenty of rest. Five days later and just two days before the new year, Eugene fell gravely ill, unable to rise from his bed, barely able to breathe. Doctors summoned to Eugene's upscale Baltimore apartment were no strangers to what they encountered. It certainly was not a cold and the reality was there was little they could do but try to make Eugene as comfortable as possible. He would either fight this off or....

While others celebrated the new year, Eugene lay in his bed, racked with fever, coughing uncontrollably at times, fighting for every breath. On January 4th 1919 he lost the fight. Eugene died from pneumonia in his apartment, surrounded by his family. He was 34 years old and although he always planned to, he never married, leaving his younger brother Herman heir to their father's fortune and legacy.

Once again Herman was devastated by the sudden loss of an older brother and dealt with his grief the only way he knew, by distracting himself with matters related to the family business, sorting Eugene's estate and now running his brother's company. Ironically Eugene's most lasting invention, a card-counting machine, was patented two years after his death. It would be the last device drafted by the Eugene Mergenthaler Company. By 1920 Herman, now a vice president with the Mergenthaler Linotype Company, had neither his brother's design nor drafting skills and had little time to oversee operations at his brother's company and was forced to close it. That same year Herman bought a home on Purchase Street in Rye, New York, not far the Connecticut border and a short train ride to the Brooklyn offices of Mergenthaler Linotype. After ten years of marriage, Alice was pregnant with their first child, and Herman wanted to raise his family in much the same manner as he was brought up, in a tranquil setting away from the crowded confines of city life. With only about five-thousand residents, Rye seemed an idyllic place with its gazeboed town green where bands played during the summer and on holidays; where trollies ran through town and where movies played at the Rye Playhouse and where in winter children skated on Mead Pond. Herman was also very familiar with the area and town, having been a long standing member and a key financial backer of the Westchester Biltmore Country Club. The property bought, their home was built not far from the club. On August 5th of that year Alice gave birth to a baby boy who, contrary to their plans and hopes, would be the couple's only child and named him after their fathers.

George Ottmar Mergenthaler was now the sole male heir to the Mergenthaler fortune.

FIVE

From the train station, Herman hopped onto a trolly that took him on the short ride to the center of town. Unless the weather said otherwise he enjoyed the twenty-minute or so walk from the train station up to their home on Purchase Street, but today he needed to stop in town to pick up a few things before heading home for the evening and the weekend. On his stroll though town, a cool March breeze accompanied him as his mind wandered aimlessly, having put to bed the day's business concerns long before arriving at the station, a self imposed rule he followed religiously. A short distance ahead the trees surrounding the town green were still bare, with only the bravest buds daring to greet the slow approach of spring. It was the patches of multicolored crocuses in full bloom surrounding the gazebo that first caught Herman's eye then, beyond the gazebo atop a small retaining wall that ran along Blind Brook, he glimpsed a young girl who looked to be a couple of years older than George, her arms stretched airplane wide, her eyes trained on her feet as she carefully placed one in front of the other. Watching her negotiate the top of the wall, and knowing she was no doubt performing in front of her thousands of fans that had come to see her in this her final attempt at Olympic gold at the Paris games, Herman couldn't help but think and smile about the dare-devil in George who, at only three years of age, seemed fearless and curious, a combination that kept Alice or their nanny on their toes most days.

Herman glanced over to see if she had indeed won her gold medal when in a blur of flailing limbs she vanished over the side of the wall. Herman dashed to the stone wall and in stride dropped his briefcase, planted his right hand onto the wall and vaulted his legs over, landing beside the motionless girl, her face half submerged in the icy water. He pulled her from the water, unconscious but breathing, and carried her up from the brook and over to a policeman's patrol car that luckily was parked nearby. Nora Mitchell arrived at the hospital in the back of the patrol car awake, frightened and wet, the knot on her head growing. She was examined by doctors who concluded that aside from a large, burgundy-red bump where her head hit rocks, she was otherwise uninjured, but they insisted on keeping her hospitalized for a short time as a precaution. Some time later Herman visited the girl to see how she was doing and presented her with a necklace as a get-well present.

George Mergenthaler age 10
Photo: Mergenthaler Family collection

That incident, combined with the Mergenthaler family history thus far, made Herman and Alice even more conscious of the fragility of life and how blessed they were with George. While they didn't want to and couldn't seal him off from the world, they would do the best they could to protect him from whatever his future held. They, especially Alice, would dote on their only child while being careful not to spoil him. Certainly his would be a life of privilege, but from the beginning they instilled in him a respect for what he had and more important for what others didn't have. When George began his grade school education at the exclusive Rye Country Day School, even at that early age he exhibited a respect and acceptance of others as well as an eagerness to please his teachers and make friends with his classmates. In short there wasn't anyone who didn't take to George. He was bright, curious, well mannered, witty, charming and more than anything displayed an insatiable thirst for learning. Early on he also showed signs of athletic ability and it was at his next school, the Canterbury School, a private, catholic, college preparatory boarding school in New Milford, Connecticut that his athletic prowess took shape. There George was a standout at squash and tennis, games he was first introduced to at an early age when he would accompany his father to the Westchester Biltmore Country Club. George took to both sports equally, but he excelled at tennis and in the summer months it was not unusual to find him on the club's pristinely manicured grass courts, sometimes playing matches against the club's best players, who often cared little about the outcome of the match but rather relished the opportunity to play against the gifted teenager. Now at Canterbury it didn't take long for George to rise above the rest of his peers and distinguish himself as the best squash and tennis player the school had seen in years.

Academically George excelled in the subjects he cared most about such as English and History, whereas in Math and Sciences, subjects he had little interest in, he had only average marks. He enjoyed the written word and was the editor of the school's weekly newspaper, *The Tabard,* and he was a contributor to the Canterbury Quarterly, the school's magazine. It was in the study of languages however that George showed the most aptitude. In the first two years at the school he took courses in Latin, French and German and recorded better than average marks in all three subjects. Although somewhat familiar with French, having studied it briefly in his last year at the Rye Country Day School, he was most familiar with German. His father, who grew up speaking German, spoke to George in German at a very early age, as did his grandmother Emma until her death in 1934, when George was 13. Although he could speak German fluently, it was formal written language and vocabulary that he was lacking. In school however his seeded language skills allowed him to easily maneuver through his language courses, leading to near native accents in both German and French, while honing his writing skills in both.

George thoroughly enjoyed his time at the school and was at ease in the academic environment, which suited and challenged him intellectually. He craved mental stimulation and engagement. He read voraciously, especially books and literature with historical threads. He had a fascination with European history and sought to absorb all he could on the topic. It was not unusual to find George in the library for long periods, skimming historical reference books and novels. Perhaps because his father had served, he had a consuming interest in the Great War now nearly twenty years ended, but still seeming not all that long ago. He was intrigued by the political, geographical, historical and cultural elements that converged at such a time and place, sparking a war unlike anything seen before, killing tens of millions of people, scarring and maiming countless souls while reducing whole cities to piles of rubble. The world had never experienced a war of this magnitude ever before and that, if nothing else, utterly fascinated George. Being of German descent and having visited his distant relatives with his father on several trips through the years he also wanted to understand more about his ancestral homeland and the role Germany had played in such a devastating world war.

When not hidden between racks of library books and losing all track of time, George reveled in the social bonding and camaraderie shared between roommates and classmates. He embraced team structure in his athletic pursuits, often spending extra time coaching tennis and squash teammates when asked. Also at Canterbury,

George's spiritual and religious devotion deepened due partly to the school's required religious studies that in turn spurred his interest in the historical roots and evolution of religions, Catholicism in particular.

School however did pose challenges for George, not the least of which was chronic sinusitis so severe it lasted for days on end and brought with it fever and piercing headaches. His sinuses were constantly blocked and that in turn led to difficulty sleeping. He spent countless nights turning from one side to the other allowing his sinuses to drain enough to allow him to breathe freely, if only for a short time.

The restless nights left him physically and mentally fatigued and would lead to trips to the school infirmary or home for days at a time. He suffered through the illness his entire first year, but the condition persisted, affecting his ability to concentrate on his studies. As his times away from class became more frequent, his grades began to suffer. Treatments of the time were ineffective and it was the Mergenthaler family physician that suggested a change to a warmer climate might be the solution to breaking the recurrence of the condition. Herman made arrangements to move George out of the Canterbury School, enrolling him for a year in the Asheville School, a private boarding school in Blue Ridge Mountains of North Carolina. His studies at Asheville would mirror those at Canterbury, and his grades would apply to his curriculum there accordingly. In just a few weeks at Asheville, George's condition began to abate and by the end of the semester it appeared to have disappeared completely. Whether the clean mountain air was the cure or George simply fought the infection is not known but the prescribed change of climate worked and George returned to the Canterbury School that following year illness free.

By June of 1939, Herman, now 53 years old, had retired from the Mergenthaler Linotype Company, while George was set to graduate second in his class from the Canterbury School, hoping to attend Princeton University in the fall. Two years earlier he had taken a prerequisite, second-level foreign language entrance exam at the university and passed easily. All that was left to do was to maintain his grades in his final year, sit for an interview and take the full entrance exams. In early April of 1939, he visited Princeton with his parents to complete the interview, leaving only exams and the official application as the final details. Upon returning to school, he immediately filled out an application, summarizing his desire to attend the Ivy League school thusly:

"The reason I am trying for Princeton is because Princeton offers courses and activities in which I am interested. I am going to college to acquire a liberal arts education. I will be able to get my degree at Princeton without Science or Mathematics, subjects which I do not like. I am interested in English and History. I hope to specialize in History in my junior and senior years and to take courses such as History of Art and Musical Appreciation. These courses at Princeton seem especially enjoyable, and I think I will like them.

I enjoy playing Squash Racquets and Tennis, sports for which Princeton has fine equipment and coaching. Besides having good athletic facilities and varied curriculum, Princeton has an atmosphere and environment that appeal to me. I like the buildings and the countryside. I think I will enjoy the social life at Princeton. I have known a number of Princeton men, and I would like to become one of them.

Yours truly,
George Ottmar Mergenthaler"

Aside from desire and academic achievement, George's acceptance may have also been attributed in part to the recommendation of Dr. Nelson Hume, headmaster of the Canterbury School who two weeks earlier in March on the "Principal's Applicant Report" requested by the University wrote:

"As a candidate for admission to Princeton, George Mergenthaler will rank in the first group. He is far above the average in intellect and personality. He had good equipment to work with and uses it. He is a boy of fine character and personality. His cultural background is unusually good, as are his family and social surroundings. His grandfather was the inventor of the Mergenthaler Linotype Machine. He has good influence on his fellow students and is well liked by them. In athletics, he is proficiently good at squash and tennis. He is our number one player in both these sports. He will undoubtedly make the teams at the University. He is now in excellent physical condition and seems to have outgrown his tendency toward sinus trouble. In every respect, Mergenthaler is a first class candidate and I recommend him without reserve."

With George's better than average grades, above average SAT score, recommendation letters, noted course interests, athletic abilities and the high scores from his entrance exams, especially his score on the recently added American History exam, a test that relied less on factual recall but instead challenged applicants to examine detailed historical facts and apply deductive reasoning to gauge the outcome of events, where George recorded one of the highest marks on record, it was not wholly unexpected that his acceptance letter arrived in late June of that year.

In September 1939, as George entered Princeton, Hitler entered Poland.

SIX

Princeton was everything George had hoped it would be and as expected he made the freshman squash team that would eventually go on to win the intercollegiate Ivy League championship that year. His upper body only now beginning to fill out, he was still lanky with rangy arms. On the court he was a chaotic flash of movement with unexpected speed and agility, the racquet seeming a natural appendage. It was those incongruently thin legs and arms that gained him the team nickname of "Moose", although most others on campus, especially close friends, gave him the nickname that would stick, simply referring to him as "Merg". Later, in his junior year and by then a dominating presence on the court, Merg played a key role in helping the nine-man varsity team go undefeated, winning the Intercollegiate Squash Association Championship held that year in Buffalo, NY and earning him a letter in that sport.

Academically, George launched into his studies by taking required college courses as well as a few electives he'd professed interest in during the application and interview process. He chose entry level classes in history and music, however in the second semester of his freshman year he dropped his introduction to music class, choosing instead a course with a particular focus on classical music, George's favorite. More often than not Merg's roommates, with whom he shared an off-campus house during his freshman year, returned from class only to be greeted at the sidewalk by Merg's classical records playing at window-rattling volumes.

As George's second year at Princeton was beginning in late summer 1940, a continent away another war in Europe was raging. Britain, France, Australia, New Zealand and Canada had all declared war on Germany while Italy, a German ally, declared war on Britain and France. Russia had invaded Finland, forcing their surrender and then invaded the Baltic States. Poland, Denmark, Belgium, Norway and by late June France, had all surrendered to Germany, leaving Britain as the last European country standing in the way of the powerful German forces. The Battle of Britain was underway with German planes and bombers at first targeting only RAF bases, airplane factories and radar installations.

Despite a war waging an ocean away, an annual poll of Princeton's incoming freshman class of 1940, conducted by the university newspaper "The Daily Princetonian", as George's class had done a year earlier, voted Adolf Hitler over Princeton's own Albert Einstein as "the greatest living person", a statement vote echoing the isolationist sentiment running through most of the country at the time. However with Britain desperately fighting for its survival, there seemed little chance of the United States remaining out of the war much longer. As Germany's Luftwaffe began pounding Britain's major cities and civilians, the United State Military Conscription Bill was passed by Congress in mid-September 1940, enabling the first peace-time draft in the country's history, with all men between the ages of 21 and 36 required to register.

Newly registered for service and seeing the events of the world unfolding, a student of history with keen foresight, George refined his studies to include classes in Politics and Art History along with a prerequisite Economics course and his continued studies in History and English. By the end of that first semester of his sophomore year he had completed all the university required courses. He had also moved on campus, sharing a room in Holder Hall, famed certainly for the Gothic architecture typical of the campus buildings of the time but more so for the 140-foot memorial tower that loomed over the dormitories' courtyard.

By the time George's second term drew to a close in early June 1941, America's involvement in the world conflict had escalated, with President Roosevelt having signed the Lend-Lease Act, thus allowing the United States to officially supply the British with military aid while the US remained tenuously neutral. That however would soon change, sealing the fates of millions of people worldwide.

George returned from Sunday mass, had a late breakfast with friends in Madison Hall, the school's main campus dining facility, and after sharing jokes and laughs followed by a more somber discussion of politics and the ever shifting flow of world events, he returned to his room to gather a few things before heading to the "South Stacks" of the library, one of his favorite retreats, to pour over history books and reference materials such as maps, letters and archived documents. Donning gold rimmed reading glasses to help lessen eye strain, George would spend hours buried in stiff-spined volumes, letting time slip away unchecked.

Today it was Napoleon's Russian campaign that garnered his attention. Certainly there was a case to be made for the repetition of history when despite the 1939 non-aggression pact between the two countries, Hitler's army invaded Russia in June of 1941. It was the same month and nearly the same day back in 1812 that Napoleon Bonaparte had marched his army of more than half a million men, at that time the largest army ever assembled, into Russia. The Russians were tenacious fighters but slowly and deliberately retreated drawing Napoleon's forces deeper into Russia. As the Russian soldiers fell back, so too did the Russian people, taking with them any supplies that may have helped the French army survive. What couldn't be carried away was destroyed or burned. Napoleon had counted on his soldiers being able to live off the conquered land as they pushed farther into Russia, since the supply system needed to support an army that large simply didn't exist. When Napoleon finally reached Moscow in September, he found most of the city engulfed in flames. Napoleon's army stayed in Moscow for more than a month, hoping an occupation of the city would prompt Tsar Alexander I to sue for peace. When no such offer came, with winter approaching and his men starving and riddled with disease, Napoleon was forced to retreat. On *this* very same day, in 1812, just six months after the campaign began, 20,000 battered and ragged soldiers, all that remained of Napoleon's once mighty army, reached the Niemen River and began crossing out of Russian territory. Considered to be a brilliant tactician, Napoleon's invasion of Russia however proved to be a military disaster, a blunder that would eventually lead to his downfall.

Only when he heard hastened foot falls echoing through the cavernous library did George glance up from Napoleon's *Grande Armée* to see his roommate F.B. Seggmeran approaching. His eyes were wide and despite the frigid December air outside, perspiration dotted his brow; his flushed face was frozen in shock. While catching his breath, Seggs relayed the news that had been crackling out of radios throughout the campus that afternoon: Pearl Harbor in the Hawaiian Island Territory, home to the US Pacific Fleet, had been attacked by the Japanese. The surprise attack lasted more than an hour and a half and dealt a crippling but not devastating blow to the fleet. Five battleships, including the USS Arizona, were sunk with three others heavily damaged. Three destroyers, three cruisers and three smaller ships were also destroyed as well as 188 aircraft. Luckily the prime targets for the Japanese, the aircraft carriers Lexington, Enterprise and Saratoga, were not in port at the time of the attack. In all more than 2400 servicemen were killed in the attack, along with 68 civilians. Nearly 1200 people were wounded. American's non-interventionist sentiment, waning since the fall of France, was about to evaporate completely. The following day, Monday, December 8th , a day after the "day that would live in infamy" as President Roosevelt coined it in an emotional address to a joint session of the US Congress, America and its ally Great Britain declared war on Japan. Three days later, on December 11th, 1941 Germany and Italy, declared war on the United States.

Following the attack on Pearl Harbor, the mood and Princeton itself changed dramatically. Waves of students swept up in patriotic fervor left school to enlist in the armed services, forcing then university president Harold Dodds to write a letter urging students to stay in school, emphasizing "the best equipment you can have for military service is a college degree and a sound physique." The plea however fell on mostly deaf ears, and enrollment continued to decline. Those remaining at Princeton saw the school quickly assume a war-time posture. Student dormitories were converted into barracks as the school was forced to open its doors for military training. Course curriculums were adjusted to include undergraduate electives in humanities and technical studies. A physical training program was established, emphasizing conditioning for war service, and by the summer of 1942, an emergency course in map-making from aerial photographs known as "photogrammetry", funded by the Department of Defense, was introduced.

Also in the summer of 1942 on July 9th, despite his father's wishes, George officially enlisted in the army and was immediately absorbed into the United States Army Enlisted Reserve Corps on campus to begin his junior year. As such, he moved into Henry Hall, one of the dormitories now converted into barracks, where he shared a room with three other students who had also enlisted. Although they still took classes with civilian students and were taught by civilian instructors, the rest of the time those in the Reserve Corps, including ROTC (Reserve Officer Training Corps) personnel, acted more as a military unit. They took meals together in Madison Hall that was now referred to as the mess hall; they marched and trained on and off campus together; they dressed in uniforms and their dormitories were subject to weekly inspections. Each morning they rose to reveille and each night they were held to a curfew. George again tailored his course load as he felt the times demanded by emphasizing history, enrolling in summer classes as part of an accelerated program, and for his last term that began in the fall of 1942 adding two elective classes: Military & Political Geography and Elementary Automotive Mechanics.

In late January of 1943, twenty-two year old George Mergenthaler, now only a few days removed from graduation, left for Camp Hood in Killeen, Texas, for basic training at the newly formed Tank Destroyer and Tactical Firing Center.

Herman and George on the campus of Princeton University, 1943 (photographed by Alice Mergenthaler)

Photo: Mergenthaler Family Collection

At the start of the war the army identified the need for mobilized weapons that could counter the seemingly unstoppable German armored units that had easily swept through Europe and into Russia. Mobile anti-tank guns on armored halftracks or special tanks were designed and built but the army needed a testing and training location with ample open space. After reviewing the list of potential sites, The War Department decided that a proposed location midway between Austin and Waco in Texas was the ideal locale. Three small towns were razed and more than 300 farming families were relocated in order for the base to be built. Construction began in April 1942, and five months later in August the first troops began arriving. Named after Confederate General John Bell Hood, commander of the Texas Brigade during the Civil War, Camp Hood officially opened a month later on September 18. Originally designed to house some 38,000 soldiers, the camp's role and size quickly expanded the following January to include an additional 40,000 acres of purchased land near Gatesville, Texas. A replacement and basic training facility initially called the sub camp but later named North Camp Hood was built to house and train an additional 40,000 troops. At the height of the war the North Camp would also house more than 4000 German POWs.

While George was going through basic training at the North Camp, he felt the pull of Tank Destroyer duty and asked to be assigned to one of the units. Meantime his father Herman worked whatever connections he could, political or otherwise, in an effort to get his son assigned stateside or, at the very least, admitted to the newly formed Army Specialized Training Program or ASTP.

George's Princeton University Yearbook picture, 1943

Photo: Mergenthaler Family Collection

(colorization: Marina Amaral)

The ASTP was developed to replace the ROTC in an effort to meet the wartime demand for both junior officers and regular soldiers with technical skills in fields such as engineering, medicine and foreign language. Newly enrolled students were expected to complete a four-year program in 18 months and exit college with a bachelor's degree and commission in hand. Since George had already graduated he would have to apply for admission and take the required entrance exam. Herman's hope was that if George was accepted into the program it would certainly delay his deployment overseas, as well as earn George a commission that would perhaps make it easier for him to be stationed stateside. Before any of that could happen however George would have to be transferred to a Specialized Training and Reassignment or "STAR" unit. Soldiers sent to STAR units underwent psychological and aptitude testing and sat for field interviews to determine their course of study and which college or university they would attend if accepted into the ASTP. For George the choice, it seemed, would be obvious: he would go back to Princeton University, one of the selected ASTP schools. However he never made it past the interview stage. The army was in need of soldiers with certain language skills and as soon as it was known that George was an Ivy League graduate who could speak fluent German and French, he was immediately designated for further specialized training. In August of 1943 George was transferred to the 28th Cavalry Reconnaissance Troop (Mechanized) stationed at Camp Pickett in Virginia along with the 28th Infantry Division to which the Recon troop had been attached. There the entire division underwent intense training while on maneuvers in the mountains of West Virginia. Three combat teams as well as George's recon troop also participated in amphibious landing training conducted by the Amphibious Force of the U.S. Atlantic Fleet at Camp Bradford, Virginia. The recon troop also received specialized training in the use of various weapons, equipment and vehicles at their disposal, tactical and deployment training, plus small unit and special combat training.

Towards the end of the time at Camp Pickett, the entire Recon Troop was granted leave to return home to their families before shipping overseas. A day's train ride later George was at home in Rye visiting with his parents, neighbors and friends. In uniform he accompanied his father and mother to the country club for a dinner hastily arranged in his honor. Always amiable and a dashing figure in uniform, his prideful parents watched as George "made the rounds" to the tables of the various club members.

"What's your unit? Where they sending you? When are they going to promote you?" were repeated queries. "Give 'em hell." "Kick some ass." and "Keep your head down," buttoned many of the table side chats. The next day Alice, with her newest camera, the one that took color photographs, made it a point to take as many photos of her son as possible before he'd have to leave again, the visit home too brief for all. At Pennsylvania Station, before boarding the train that would eventually have him back at Camp Pickett before sundown, he once again promised he'd

George in the yard of the Mergenthaler home in Rye, NY, September 1943. Photographed by his mother.

Photo: Mergenthaler Family collection

write as often as he could. Herman handed his son a small box, a going away present of a kind, but told him to open it later. George took a seat by a window and looked at the box. A loud hiss and jolt from the train jarred him away from his thoughts as the train pulled away from the station. He jumped to his feet, opened the window, poked his head out, and then smiled wide and waved goodbye to his parents.

Six weeks after they first arrived at Camp Pickett, the entire division, including the Recon Troop, boarded trains that would take them north to Camp Myles Standish in Taunton, Massachusetts, just outside of Boston. Named after the English military officer who arrived with the Pilgrims on the Mayflower in 1620 and who later became the first military commander of the Plymouth Colony, the camp officially opened in October 1942. Its sole purpose was to serve as a departure holding area for troops preparing to be shipped overseas. The 28th Infantry Division would spend ten days at the camp before finally assembling at Pier 5 in Boston Harbor on October 8th 1943 and boarding the SS Santa Rosa for the trans-Atlantic journey.

SEVEN

Known as the "Keystone" Division because of their distinctive red keystone shoulder patches, the same keystone symbol of Pennsylvania Army National Guard hailing from the "Keystone State" and the oldest division in the United States Armed Forces, the 28th Infantry Division can trace its lineage back to Benjamin Franklin's battalion during the Revolutionary War. Officially established in 1879 it was later designated as the 28th Infantry when America entered into World War One in 1917. The division arrived in Europe in May of 1918 and began training with the British, but it was in July that the 28th distinguished itself on the battlefield, earning fame and honor. While assuming defensive positions along the Marne River east of Chateau-Thierry, the Germans commenced a vicious attack with a punishing artillery bombardment designed to weaken the American line. Once the barrage lifted, German troops attacked with speed and in force, slamming into the main body of the 28th. The fighting was brutal and before long was hand-to-hand. The American soldiers fought valiantly, holding the line again and again and eventually repelled the German attack. The battle over, Gen. John "Black Jack" Pershing, in command of the American Expeditionary Force, visited the battlefield, and after seeing the carnage and the surviving soldiers, proclaimed the 28th Infantry division "Men of Iron" and named the 28th his "Iron Division."

Attached to the 28th Division, the 28th Cavalry Recon Troop's role was an update to older horse cavalry units. At strength of 160 men the troop was broken down into a headquarters platoon and three additional line platoons. Each of those platoons was further divided into three squadrons, each outfitted with an M-8 armored car equipped with a .30 caliber machine gun, a .50 caliber machine gun and a 37mm turret mounted cannon capable of firing either armor piercing shells or anti-personnel shells. The squads were also equipped with at least one mortar jeep and one machine gun jeep, a command jeep and a radio jeep as well as basic transport vehicles and halftracks. Additionally each squadron was assigned a medic from the 103rd Medical Battalion. Unlike the infantry division to which they were attached, the recon troop's primary mission was not to engage the enemy in combat but rather to move in advance of the main fighting force to assess enemy strength, position and movement. Whatever information they gathered was then sent back to the command center, either by radio or messenger and then relayed to G-2, the army's intelligence arm for analysis and to plan a course of action. Due to the fluid nature of war however, enemy engagements were often unavoidable. As one Recon Troop veteran would later recall, "sometimes the only way to locate the enemy was to keep going until someone starting shooting at you."

Ten days after leaving Boston harbor, the Recon Troop along with the rest of the division arrived in Swansea, Wales, on the afternoon of October 18th. The next day, they boarded troop transport trucks that would take them to destinations deeper into Wales to begin their training for the eventual invasion of Europe. Due to its size, the entire division was scattered over a wide area in western Wales, making aggressive training in large numbers difficult. Plus with additional units continuing to arrive, many troops had to be relocated frequently and with the limited training areas in high demand by all divisions, some training was restricted to small unit exercises, marksmanship and physical conditioning. Part of that physical conditioning included long marches in full combat gear through the Welsh countryside. However there was one area where troops received extensive and the most beneficial training; at the US Army Assault Training Center in Woolacomb, England. There soldiers engaged in individual and small unit exercises in various combat skills, including amphibious landings and assaults on fortified positions under "live fire" conditions that included the use of artillery and naval bombardment.

George and the rest of the Recon Troop rolled through the town of St. Clears on the afternoon of October 19th, 1943. The town saddled the swift flowing, always rain swollen River Taf that stretched more than twenty feet wide in some places, while meandering through billiard table green pastures and wetlands of the Welsh countryside, its waters spilling into an expansive estuary near the ruins of Laugharne Castle on the eastern side of Carmarthen Bay. Remnants of the morning's only-threatening high clouds retreated southward towards the bay, the setting sun seizing precious moments to paint them a vibrant flame orange; a welcome gesture for the soldiers of "Hotdog" as they made their way to their new home for the next several months, the grounds of Pen y Coed mansion, a 17th century country great house located two miles outside of town, that overlooked some of those same lush pastures, farmers fields and river wetlands.

Chosen as the unit headquarters for the Recon Troop, the men would take their meals in any of the mansion's large rooms now converted into make-shift mess halls on the ground floor, while upper echelon officers and any visiting dignitaries would be housed in rooms on the mansion's upper floors. Meantime the rest of the recon soldiers were billeted in Quonset huts erected on the spacious grounds surrounding the mansion. The semicircular cross-sectioned, prefabricated structures of corrugated, galvanized steel, modeled after the Nissen huts first developed by the British during the first world war, took their name from Quonset Point in North Kingstown, Rhode Island, where they were first manufactured. Lightweight and easy to assemble, each twenty by forty foot hut provided 720 square feet of floor space. Insulated inside, with doors and windows at either end of the hut and with a pressed wood floor, they made for ideal barracks once the soldiers became accustomed to the sound of the rain pinging against the huts' steel shells. It was loud, but dry. Originally designed to comfortably hold up to twenty soldiers, the Quonset huts would be pushed to their space limits with each hut housing thirty and even forty soldiers.

Because of his education and language skills, George had been assigned to the headquarters platoon, where he met a soldier from Marinette, Wisconsin, named Cletus LaFond. Cletus, the younger of the two sons of George and Marie Lafond, always received better than average grades in school, and it was during high school that he taught himself how to use a typewriter, eventually becoming proficient at it. Classmates marveled at how Cletus' fingers appeared to flow over the rows of letters, producing pages of neat copy with few mistakes. Using money he earned while working as a caddy at the local golf club during the summer months, he eventually bought a Royal typewriter in hopes of furthering a writing career. Upon graduating high school he applied and was accepted to the University of Wisconsin but left after only one semester to help support the family that was still struggling in the wake of the great depression a decade earlier. Cletus went to work for a furniture manufacturing company, his dreams of a writing career stalled first by work and then by war. In October of 1942, Cletus enlisted and due in part to his typing skills, found himself assigned to the 28th Cavalry Reconnaissance Troop headquarters company as a clerk, tasked with typing after action reports, official orders, record keeping and should the need arise, letters from the commanding officers to the families of soldiers killed, wounded or missing in action.

Cletus matched George in height, was slim, square jawed and

shouldered with a lean, athletic build. He had thick black hair that slid back from a widow's peak, leaving a face often graced by a high-cheeked, magazine cover-worthy smile. Some said he looked like Errol Flynn, the swashbuckling movie star. George and Cletus had met during training at Camp Pickett, and despite the unlikely match of the jocose, spirited and sociable George and Cletus who, despite his better-than-average good looks, at times seemed diffident, reticent and occasionally socially ill at ease, the two became fast friends. It may have been his boundless enthusiasm and optimism, his intrinsic desire to fully embrace all that life had to offer regardless of circumstance, his resolute hopefulness, his infectious charm and quick wit, or perhaps his gentleness and kindness that drew him in, but regardless Cletus took an immediate liking to George. He was not alone. Everyone in the unit seemed to immediately take to George. At best, other men wanted to emulate him, at least be included in his sphere. Women it seemed, desperately wanted to be noticed by him. For Cletus, his shyness and reserve quickly evaporated whenever he was with George.

Despite his father's best intentions, George was adamant about entering the service as a buck private. There would be no privilege or influence here, and he was guarded about his upbringing, his family background and the fortune waiting for him after the war. Save for his Princeton education, his hometown in Rye, and only the most basic information about his mother, father and grandparents, the rest of his personal story he kept private. Yet with Cletus, George found someone whom he could talk to and joke with for hours without ever running out of conversation. From the moment they met, George immediately felt comfortable talking with Cletus about anything and everything. He could be himself; no need to shy away from his family background. For some reason he couldn't explain an immediate trusting bond developed. While the rest of the men in the troop knew only surface details of George's background, that he came from a well-to-do family and that his grandfather was an inventor of some sort, it was with

Cletus after dinner at the mansion one night, over coffee and Lucky Strikes, that George let Cletus into his family.

If Cletus was at all impressed or intimidated by Mergenthaler's good fortune, he never let it show. As far as he was concerned, Merg was just another soldier thrown into the horrible circumstance of war. George and Cletus, along with fellow headquarters platoon soldiers Sgt. Charles Stansbury from East Aurora, New York; Cpl. George Raduykavich from Pittsburgh, PA; Cpl. Joe Vocasek from Kansas and Staff Sgt. Richard Sheesley from New York, were shoe-horned into the tight living quarters along with second and third Platoon soldiers, Cpl. Charles "Chuck" Jones from Maryland, Pvt. Gene McHale from Virginia, Cpl. Kenneth Knapp from Middletown, NY, Cpl. John Kost from Bethlehem, PA, Pvt. Maloy "MC" Joiner from Tennessee; SSgt. Chandler Capps from Kannapolis, North Carolina; Sgt. Daniel Garbo from Illinois; Cpl. Loyd Griffin from Georgia and Pvt. Fred Linden from Ohio.

Privacy was at a premium and for George it meant sharing every package from home, but especially the seemingly always arriving packages sent by his mother, the ones containing cakes and cookies that were eagerly and happily devoured by all around. In fact it was Cpl. Joe Vocasek, a fleshy faced, pugnacious soldier with a raspy voice and the throaty laugh of a smoker, serving as the company mailman, who would alert the others in the troop whenever George received packages from home. The return address of the Commodore Hotel, from where Herman would mail most of the packages knowing that he could rely on the hotel's influence to assure the packages would arrive in the shortest time possible, was enough to cause a stir amongst the troop. It shocked no one that George blithely shared whatever he had, even if it was only baked treats. While he poured over the latest edition of the Princeton Alumni Weekly and other magazines thoughtfully sent by his mother, the rest of the soldiers helped themselves to whatever was in those tins, the contents never lasting long. The closeness of the huts also meant the soldiers often received one-on-one German lessons from George. Not long after their arrival in Wales, George had been tapped to teach German to officers and non-commissioned soldiers as well. Formal classes were held regularly at Pen y Coed mansion where basic German phrases, the ones any soldier might need once deployed in the country, were taught. It was the informal setting in those huts however, when teaching German and French to any soldier eager to learn, that George was most at ease and himself, giving to those who didn't have.

During their time in the huts the soldiers were also resupplied with new uniforms, new weapons and other equipment needed for their individual assignments or areas of specialized training, and the Recon Troop as a whole was outfitted with new vehicles for training that would eventually follow them across the English channel, including M-8 armored cars, half-tracks, jeeps and a 2-1/2 ton truck.

As the buildup to the invasion continued, more soldiers began arriving into the area, forcing most of the Recon Troop to be relocated out of the Quonset huts and into a large barn on Pen y Coed mansion grounds while some in the group were scattered amongst homes, barns and abandoned buildings in and around the town of St. Clears. Billeted in a room on the upper floor of a home not far from the center of town overlooking the river were Merg, Cletus, Joe Vocasek and M-8 driver Charles Stansbury, a rose-cheeked, farm-fresh faced soldier of average build with a tight weave of sandy blond hair, who often said little, content to absorb all that was around, soaking in the new experiences brought on by his army life and the first time he'd been away from home.

The room was small with just enough space for the four men to find a spot for their army-issued cots, their gear and little else. Two small windows on the eastern wall of the room overlooked a small field that at the far end gave way to a gentle bend in the river. A small coal burning firebox on the north wall fueled by the soldiers' allotment of coal for the week was the only source of heat. If the nights turned too cold and if the soldiers had used up their weekly coal allotment, they went without heat until the next week. There was no electricity but each morning the men were greeted by the constant and soothing call of the river spilling over time-smoothed stones that, to their ears, sounded remarkably similar to small waves breaking on a beach. The house was also a short walk to nearby restaurants and pubs where the men sought refuge from aching, blistered feet courtesy of army issued boots and the rolling Welsh hills. For George it was just a brisk 15 minute walk to the steps of St. Mary Magdalene church, where he attended mass daily to receive communion, for as he wrote in his last letter to his parents before boarding the troop ship in Boston harbor, "There really isn't anything to worry about, and with a good confession under your belt nothing is terrible."

Although they had little choice, the townspeople in St. Clears were welcoming, sharing what they had and opening their homes to the uniformed strangers in a strange land destined for still stranger lands someday from which they may never to return. Fridays in town was fish and chips from five to seven followed by dancing in the nearby dance hall with music courtesy of local bands such as The Melody Makers, comprised of townspeople. Sometimes members from the 28th Infantry Division band, sent into surrounding towns to entertain the troops, would play. Local girls delighted in attending the dances and meeting the wonderfully different American soldiers, while the local lads stood little chance against the cadre of sharply uniformed GIs eagerly spending money throughout the tiny town. Whisky, if lucky enough to find some, was the drink of choice, but most settled for warm, flat beer until last call.

"Time Gentlemen", Military Police bellowed across the layers of smoke and din at the stroke of 10pm. Soldiers learned quickly to get their last pull from the tap just before the call, allowing them to stay longer to finish their beer and remain with their dates. Rules often slackened once the MPs moved on.

Soldiers were routinely invited to the homes of the townspeople they'd befriended for Sunday dinner, the understanding being that the soldiers had to supply the main course. Cletus and Merg, as he was once again nick-named, often made deals with company cooks, swapping this for that; five pound tins of Spam magically appeared. It's all they had and for what they had, soldiers and their host families ate well those days. And it was at those dinners that Cletus was always taken with Merg's ability to engage in conversation with anyone, on any subject, for what seemed like hours. The weather, the farms, the town and its history, the river, the church and of course the war were all in play. What impressed Cletus the most was Merg's genuine interest in the people of St. Clears, in how they lived, what they did, what they hoped to do. Merg's gift of conversation was rooted in his ability to listen more than speak. Merg asked questions, then listened deeply and at length to the answer, nodding, smiling, absorbing. In that listening came an understanding of the people he had met, a connection made. Merg never forgot a name and always tucked away some detail that passed during the course of conversations, a mental note retrieved days or weeks later, the connection emphasized. Such was the case that one dinner when the scarcity of silk was mentioned in passing.

"It's not a must-have, mind you, still it'd be nice. Perhaps for the sleeves or the neckline or as a bit of trim. It *is* her wedding day after all but naturally she understands what with the war and all," lamented Mrs. Hart on the making of her daughter Joan's wedding dress. It was the one that she wore all those years ago that would be restitched as needed, changed for the more modern times, the one that would have to be simple but tasteful, befitting the blessed event planned for later next spring, perhaps in May or June. Surely the war would be over by then, or so they hoped. Weeks later, again invited for Sunday dinner, Merg once again arrived with the tin of Spam in hand and with a newly arrived package from home tucked under his arm.

It was with children that Merg seemed most at ease. Perhaps because he was an only child, never having had a brother or sister, he found great pleasure talking to the children, playing their games or sitting with them while they showed him their toys. He was gentle, kind and generous with his attention and with whatever treats he could scrounge up, including army-issued chocolate or with whatever he could buy in the shops in London while on leave or with what he could convince his mother to send over, tinned cakes squirreled away from the troop, a quickly devoured favorite.

When not chatting with the locals, Merg, as well as other soldiers, took advantage of other activities on offer, including visits to the local cinema. The doors opened at five in the afternoon, and GIs usually packed in to watch newly arrived training films, the latest newsreels and in most cases re-watch Chester Morris starring as Horatio "Boston Blackie" Black, the suave criminal-turned-freelance detective, fighting crime while dancing along the line of the law himself. There were a half-dozen movies in the series, each running just over an hour long and playing in rotation at the cinema Monday through Friday. Once Boston Blackie solved the crime and the GIs found out "who done it", they went for chow and afterwards took to the pubs to drink their fill, throw darts, play cards or gamble on dice games. Money changed hands; winners drank free, losers drank more. The centrally located Black Lion Pub, with a bar that stretched nearly the entire width of the building and a small seating area to the left of the bar furnished with a few well worn tables and chairs and sporting a large stone fireplace, was a favorite GI haunt. It was also where 18-year old Emma Friar and her friends came when they had the not-too-often chance.

Working as a "Land Girl", Emma came from London as a member of the Women's Land Army, later referred to as the forgotten army. Wearing uniforms of green sweaters and ties and brown felt hats and coveralls, these young girls came from all over the UK to work farming jobs vacated by men turned soldiers. The minimum age for a Land Girl was 17 but many lied about their age to be accepted into the program. They came mostly from the surrounding rural communities, but more than a third came from cities like London, where German bombs continued to wreak indiscriminate devastation on the civilian population. Most of the girls had little to no farming experience but were determined to do their part and worked planting and harvesting crops, tending to livestock and delivering milk from sun up until sun down doing their part to help feed the nation; to survive the war.

It was on one of those Saturday nights that Emma and some of her fellow Land Girls in need of a break from farm chores journeyed into St. Clears for pints at the Black Lion. Not long after they arrived Sgt. Dan Garbo struck up a conversation with the girls, with young Emma catching his eye. At that moment for the two of them everyone else and everything else, the din of the pub, the soaking rain that fell outside and especially the reason both of them found themselves in Wales at all, ceased to exist. At that moment there was only them, locked in conversation, their immediate and mutual attraction palpable, the night proving much too short. For the rest of the time he was in St. Clears, Sgt. Garbo made it a point to visit Emma whenever he could. While others in the troop spent their time on leave exploring other parts of Wales, Scotland or London, Dan Garbo spent his time stealing away with Emma whenever and wherever he could. Young and in love, their passion was overwhelming in a time of war and uncertainty. Dan and Emma shared every moment of free time together, both knowing it would end sometime but neither wanting that time to arrive. Whenever he couldn't be with Emma, Dan would write, sometimes short notes to let her know she was in his thoughts, but most times long letters professing his love and the future he hoped the two would someday share. It was in one of those letters that Dan Garbo made Emma a promise: that if he survived the war he would return to find her.

When they didn't head into town, the soldiers of the Recon Troop were often entertained by Merg in the barn at the Pen y Coed mansion, who with his short army-cut hair combed forward and a black tape or comb-end mustache, broke into wild imitations of Hitler, complete with absurdly thick-accented blustery speeches, thrashing gestures, wild eyes and the occasional bout of goose-stepping.

Sometimes the soldiers laughed so hard they nearly wet themselves.

Christmas 1943 brought turkey, ice cream and beer to soldiers who knew they'd be spending the holiday together rather than home with their families and Merg took it upon himself to keep their spirits up. After dinner, with beer flowing, Hitler arrived wearing a Santa hat and a white beard, the black-tape mustache fully visible. Santa Adolf goose-stepped in carrying a sack loaded with wrapped gifts and singing a fiery, unforgettable version of "Jingle Bells". After the song ended and the laughter subsided, the boys in the Recon Troop each received a small, token gift from Santa Adolf: gifts that had been thought about and chosen for each man well in advance when Santa asked those on leave in London to pick up a certain item if possible, or when he went into town, shopping at the local stores, or when he received packages of requested items from home. For being in a strange land, far from home and family at this special time of year, as the war to which they knew they'd soon be called raged beyond the eastern shore and across the channel, none could think of a better way to have spent the holiday.

Soldiers of the 28th Cavalry Reconnaissance Troop (Mechanized) photographed at Pen y Coed Mansion in Wales, March 1944.

(George Mergenthaler is the last soldier on the right in the back row)

Photo: National Archives

After the turn of the new year George was finally granted an extended leave and in mid February 1944 visited London once again. With time to spend he was able to meet English friends he'd known while attending Princeton. They often met for lunch or dinner at the well known Constitutional Club just steps from Trafalgar Square. Distinctive with its red and yellow, highly detailed, Victorian Neo-Gothic terra-cotta design, the club was established in the late 1800's and was a mainstay of the conservatives of English government. George however found his friends and the others he met there "quite progressive" and deeply interested in the exchange of ideas, political philosophies and culture between the US and England, especially considering courses at Princeton that were still being offered to English servicemen. All agreed that the exposure to each-other's cultures does more to cement understandings between the two countries than any written propaganda could possibly achieve. George made their point noting that even in the last few months that he and his fellow soldiers had been in Wales, and although most of those soldiers did not have George's world exposure, their experiences to date had undoubtedly given them a greater appreciation for the Welsh culture, a culture no doubt tested by the presence of swarms of American GIs training for war.

George spent a good deal of his time in London in the role of a tourist, taking in the sights of the historic city now draped in the fabric of war. Everywhere were reminders of the ongoing Luftwaffe attacks: charred-black shells of buildings; people walking around and in some cases over piles of rubble on their way to work or home; areas of the city without running water or electricity; parts of the London Underground closed because of bomb damage, windows taped to prevent shattering; nighttime blackouts; air raid sirens and government and critical buildings guarded and well sandbagged.

Despite the rich history London had to offer, George's attention was focused more on the resilience of a people that had endured years of what must have seemed like endless nights huddled below ground not knowing if they would live to see the morning as German bombs fell above. No longer just newspaper or magazine accounts, or reports heard on the radio, George now saw firsthand the devastation of the war. He returned from leave refreshed in mind and body and with a renewed spirit determined to do whatever he could, no matter how small, to defeat the enemy and bring the war to an end.

In mid April, 1944, after more than six months in Wales, the division was ordered east to an army base in England. The day the people of St. Clears and the soldiers knew would come someday finally did. Nearly everyone turned out, lining the streets to say goodbye to the soldiers as they marched to the train depot. Gifts and addresses were exchanged, hugs given, tears flowed. During his time in town George had become a son to some, a grandson to others, an older brother or a dear friend. Watching George and the others leave town was one of the saddest days anyone in St. Clears could recall during the entire war. Other soldiers would eventually arrive to replace the 28th Recon Troop, but their presence just wasn't the same. Perhaps because they were the first to arrive or perhaps it was the soldiers themselves that were in some way different than those that would follow, but whatever the reason, to the people in St. Clears the soldiers of the Recon Troop were truly special and left their lasting mark on the town and its people that would never forget them.

Arriving in Tidworth, England the Recon Troop soldiers were now billeted at a converted peacetime British cavalry barracks where they were finally able to sleep on beds with springs and real mattresses, take endless hot showers and dine on hot food in the battalion size mess hall that was outfitted with a full kitchen. No more were company cooks forced to prepare limited meals on makeshift field stoves. Compared to the cramped living conditions in Wales, this was easy time. In town there was a movie theater, restaurants and pubs, all of which the soldiers were encouraged to frequent when they first arrived. However a couple of weeks after they arrived the division and base went into "lock-down" mode: no leaves were granted and no passes to town were issued. Outfitted with their full complement of vehicles, "Hot Dog" ramped-up their training and readiness for what everyone knew was the imminent invasion of Occupied Europe. For the next four weeks the Recon Troop practiced amphibious landings and deployment, trained for town by town and house by house warfare, practiced tactical maneuvers throughout the countryside, rehearsed marshaling for the invasion, prepped their personal and troop equipment, studied maps as best they could considering all the town names were purposely left off the charts to ensure secrecy, and they attended orientation lectures and presentations designed to prepare them for what they would encounter once in France and beyond. What no one outside of high command knew was the exact location and timetable for the invasion, codenamed Operation Overlord.

As the buildup of men and equipment mounted, elaborate deceptions were underway in hopes of fooling and confusing German defenders as to where and when the invasion would take place. Codenamed Operation Quicksilver, an entire phantom army, the First United States Army Group supposedly under the command of Gen. George Patton, complete with fake tanks, artillery pieces, trucks, jeeps, planes and ships together with simulated radio traffic and troop movements, was "assembled" in and around Kent, England, the shortest point across the notoriously choppy English Channel to the Pas de Calais in France. Strategically an invasion here made the most sense as it would provide a quick turnaround time for supporting ships and air cover and provide the quickest route into Germany. It was therefore the key deception that the Allies hoped would fool the Germans, although plans for other fake invasions were leaked through double agents, together with false radio traffic, that indicated possible landings in areas of the western Mediterranean, the Balkans, the Bay of Biscay and Norway.

Finally, as May succumbed to a stormy June start, troops were moved to the actual invasion launch areas in Dover and Dorset.

Originally scheduled to launch on June 5th, rough weather caused a delay of 24 hours making June 6th, 1944 D-Day and 6:30 H-Hour, the time when the largest amphibious military assault in history, consisting of more than 156,000 American, British and Canadian troops, landed on a 50-mile stretch of heavily defended beach in Normandy region of France.

Held in reserve, it would be another month before the 28th Infantry Division finally moved to marshaling areas near Southampton on July 18th. Finally they boarded the *SS Belva Lockwood* troop carrier, and after being tossed about on rough seas during the 115 mile English Channel crossing, they landed on Omaha Beach in Normandy on July 24th. For the next six days the Recon Troop bivouacked inland near the French town of Colombières. Here, reunited with their motorized equipment, the soldiers made final preparations before entering into combat. On July 30th the Recon Troop, along with the rest of the 28th Infantry Division, moved through the French countryside to an area south of St. Lo known as the "bocage" region. A patchwork of long-standing farmers' fields defined by tall trees and tightly clustered hedgerows with masses of thick ancient roots packed with hardened earth making them as dense and formidable as any fence or wall, it made movement through this area slow and dangerous. Aerial reconnaissance photographs failed to adequately show the denseness of the hedgerows, and despite their thorough training in nearly all types of warfare they were expected to encounter, the soldiers were not prepared for this plodding advance. The overgrown hedges provided more than ample coverage for enemy defenders. From concealed positions just beyond the hedges, rifles and machine guns opened up on the advancing soldiers, catching them in deadly crossfires. Mortar positions to the rear of the machine gunners lobbed shells onto GIs who desperately sought cover in the rutted country roads, while German tanks prowled open fields and roads. Snipers in various well concealed vantage points had their pick of targets. Ground gains were measured in yards; losses in blood.

Merg, Cletus and the rest of the Recon Troop, in the lead for the 110th regiment, were forced to alter their tactics to adapt to the slow pace of the attack. Their M-8 vehicles, unable to move with speed through the rutted, hedgerow-lined roads, proved easy targets for the German tanks or from soldiers firing the deadly and highly effective single-shot Panzerfaust anti-tank weapon. The Recon Troop was forced to cautiously enter sectors in jeeps, then advance on foot into an area well ahead of the main attack force, doing their best to identify German strongholds and positions. This often meant engaging the enemy to properly locate their positions. Once located and marked, the Recon Troops would fall back and relay the map coordinates of enemy positions to the command center, either by radio or by messenger. Armed with the information provided, artillery and troop movements were adjusted for maximum effect. The Germans however also adapted and would allow the smaller reconnaissance forces to pass by unchecked hoping to ensnare the larger mass of troops that would no doubt follow when given the "all clear" from the advance scouts. It was a strategy that worked all too often and all too well. Still, owing to relentless determination combined with improvised battlefield tactics and soldier ingenuity, the division was able to make slow but steady progress forcing the Germans to give up ground. Finally, after ten days of fierce fighting the division broke out from the "bocage" region and by the end of July Merg's Recon Troop rolled up to the outskirts of the town of Percy. Once there however their advance was halted by pockets of ardent German defenders, including devastating sniper fire. Paused at the edge of town while they radioed details of their situation back to headquarters, the Germans hit back with a sudden mortar attack on their position, immediately taking out the lead M-8, killing the driver and radioman inside and two additional soldiers who were standing near the vehicle. The rest of the troop pulled back from the town and waited for the rest of the infantry to arrive. To their surprise it was a group of MPs attached to the 28th Infantry Division that arrived first. The MPs had no intention of waiting and took to the streets of Percy to clear out the remaining Germans. An intense building to building fight for the town ensued, and it was on August 1 that the Americans finally took the town that was now reduced to rubble and bombed out buildings.

From here the Recon Troop and the division pivoted eastward. Free from the constant yoke of hedgerow cluttered fields and oxen-cart wide roads, they were able to move steadily but cautiously along narrow roads, chasing the Wehrmacht back towards Germany. Montbray, Montguoray, Gathemo and St Sever de Calvados were the next in a series of towns to be liberated.

As the fighting opened up and the 28th Infantry Division began making sizable gains in territory, the mission of the Recon Troop varied day to day and in some cases hour by hour. While sometimes serving as principle contact with flanking units, or conducting motorized "mop-up" patrols in fringe regions, or serving as rear guards and establishing roadblocks, the Recon Troop mostly stayed on point for rapidly advancing columns of infantry soldiers, reconnoitering and clearing the way forward while acting as intelligence scouts and sending frontline reports directly to divisional command. With the Recon Troop out in front it was Merg, always riding in the command jeep, who was usually the first to make contact with townspeople. His command of French allowed him to easily get information on German strengths and positions in and around the towns. In some instances, the Germans had retreated well before the Recon Troop arrived into what was left of the bomb-ravaged towns. When that was the case, the Recon Troop quickly dispatched a messenger to relay the information to command while the rest of the Recon Troop would take up defensive positions and wait for the infantry to arrive in relief.

By mid-August the 28th Infantry Division had turned north and was racing toward the Seine River. Here the division advanced miles at a time in troop trucks rolling on paved roads, carving their way through the French countryside. Gathering along the roads the French came out to welcome and cheer on the soldiers, waving hands and flags, tossing flowers and apples to their American liberators. From the passing trucks the GIs tossed chocolate, Life Savers candies and cigarettes to the admiring crowds.

The spirited welcome received by the truckloads of GIs paled to that received by the men of the Recon Troop. With the divisional regiments now mechanized and advancing rapidly, it was the mission of the Recon Troop to head out well in advance of the main convoy and provide protective screens along the roads and small towns ahead. They were also able to gather intelligence on the fleeing Germans and evaluate the likelihood of counter attacks on ripe targets: truckloads of infantry soldiers. As such the men of "Hot Dog" arrived into newly-liberated areas well ahead of the main force and were greeted by adoring townspeople eager to welcome allied soldiers bringing long anticipated freedom. It was during these times that Merg easily negotiated on behalf of the rest of the troop, trading whatever they had with the townspeople for wine or liquor, cheeses, apples and bread. After years of Nazi occupation the overjoyed French were more than happy to share whatever they could with their American liberators. Liberation however came at a steep price, with most of these towns reduced to nothing more than piles of smoldering rubble with people who chose to stay rather than flee now dead in the aftermath of the fierce fighting.

By late August Allied forces were racing towards Paris trapping large portions of the German Seventh Army in a pincer-like maneuver around the town of Falaise. In what became known as the Falaise Pocket, the British Army driving south from Caen and the First US Army pushing east attempted to cut off the Wehrmacht withdrawal from the region. As the Germans retreated the 28th Infantry Division turned north, hoping to keep the remnants of the German Seventh Army from quickly retreating eastward and crossing the Seine.

On August 22nd the Recon Troop was tasked with reconnoitering the town of Le Neubourg, located just west of Seine. A vital transportation hub Northwest of Paris, Le Neubourg served as the headquarters for the German army in that sector and was expected to be heavily fortified. Anticipating this, the Americans considered bypassing the town, both to prevent a prolonged and costly fight and to hurry toward the town of Elbeuf, with hopes of further halting the German withdraw across the Seine. It was the Recon Troop's job to gather as much intelligence as possible to determine German strength and defensive positions and allow command to decide the best strategy for taking the town.

Shortly before midnight, a platoon from the Recon Troop including Merg and Cletus, as well as Pvt. Charles Stansbury and Pvt. Gene McHale, a radio operator from Maryland, arrived on the outskirts of town. Through thick fog and over rain-soaked terrain, they crept as close to the town as they dared, stopping at the sound of German voices from forward outposts. Despite the steady drizzle, they decided to remain in position on a small ridge overlooking Le Neubourg until sunrise. As morning broke splashing light onto the town, out from the retreating clouds came German fighter planes flying low in the grey eastern sky, making bombing runs, targeting roadways, bridges and, it seemed to the Recon platoon nested on the ridge, anything else where the plane's pilots expected advancing troops to be positioned.

Their payloads spent, the planes then made several passes over the countryside strafing targets of opportunity. Luckily the Recon platoon's ridge position, although somewhat exposed to aircraft, was too close to town and near German positions, preventing them from being spotted let alone targeted by the Luftwaffe pilots.

Finally around 7:00AM, as the rumbling planes disappeared eastward, the Recon soldiers, soaked to the skin, took advantage of the overhead diversion and the now vacated German outposts and quickly sprinted into the sleepy town. They moved swiftly but cautiously, checking around corners, points high and low, their months of training tested with every step. Moving through street after street the soldiers were soon dumbstruck not by the lack of enemy contact but by the lack of enemy altogether. As they approached what appeared to be the town center, from one of the buildings walling the road, a door opened. The men froze and held their breaths, rifles aimed and ready. From the doorway stepped a man who, with his time lined and days unshaven face, and wearing a well worn linen shirt and suspended trousers, couldn't be anything else but a Frenchman. He was startled at the sight of the American soldiers, their weapons trained. Merg immediately spoke to the man in French, hoping to put him and the GIs at ease. Momentarily surprised by the French speaking soldier, the man looked them over, and then smiled.

"Les Americains" he blurted out, clearly not concerned about his words echoing along the otherwise deserted street. "Boche kaputt", he quickly followed with a shrug and sneer.

Merg continued talking to the man, gathering any information he could, while the others nervously scanned the surrounding buildings. After the brief exchange he relayed what the man had said, confirming what the soldiers by this time had already assumed: overnight most of the German headquarter forces had withdrawn from Le Neubourg. The scout platoon immediately left town as fast as they could to deliver the news. Still under strict radio silence, it was decided that Pvt. McHale would take a jeep and personally deliver a hand written message to the divisional headquarters. Upon arriving, McHale handed the note to General George Davis, second in command.

"Yes!" Davis blurted out through a toothy smile, while slashing at the air with a sort of victory hand-chopping gesture. "Soldier," he steadied looking squarely at Pvt. McHale, "can you hold that town until I can get some infantry up there?"

Confusion washed across McHale's face, not because of the question but rather by the situation, that being a Brigadier General asking a buck private to assess whether a few dozen men from a reconnaissance troop could hold a town for who knows how long, against a possible German counter attack comprised of God knows how many enemy troops. After half a moment's pause McHale straightened, snapped a salute and replied boldly, "Yes sir!"

Thirty-six hours later the infantry arrived to relieve the Recon Troop, but not before the troop had knocked out three enemy troop trucks and captured two dozen soldiers including an officer and his driver. For their actions in Le Neubourg "Hot Dog" was awarded the Croix de Guerre unit citation.

The relatively easy success of the Recon Troop in Le Neubourg would not be shared by the rest of the division. German command anticipated the allied advance and pincer maneuver and was determined not to let what happened in Falaise happen again. The Germans chose to withdraw from Le Neubourg and establish a defensive line outside the town Elbeuf located just west of the Seine. German Panzer tanks and scattered but well entrenched infantry held off rapidly advancing regiments of the 28th infantry division long enough for what remained of the German Seventh Army to board barges and cross the Seine. For the next day and a half, intense fighting raged and casualties mounted as the 28th pushed forward with infantry, field artillery, tank destroyer and armor units, eventually punching through the German defenses and liberating Elbeuf on August 25th. The fight won, the battle-hardened 28th turned south toward Paris.

EIGHT

Excitement and anticipation pulsed through the streets of Paris with the promise of another parade through the Arc de Triomphe and down the Champs-Élysées. Two days earlier on August 26th, French General Charles de Gaulle and soldiers from the French 2nd Armor division triumphantly marched down the avenue to mark the official liberation of Paris, even as pockets of German resistance held firm in parts of the city and snipers perched on rooftops took pot shots at de Gaulle. Tomorrow however, on the 29th of August, almost four years to the day in 1940 when conquering German soldiers further humiliated a defeated France by marching in lockstep down the famous boulevard, an even larger spectacle would take place when the entire 28th Infantry Division would parade in review before General de Gaulle, General Omar Bradley, General Courtney H. Hodges and all of Paris.

For seventeen year old Anne Beaussier, it would be the most excitement she'd witnessed since six months earlier, beginning on the 6th of March when thick black smoke, foul and pungent, began pouring from the chimney of the 19th century three story house directly across the street from where she lived at number 20 Rue le Sueur. People living in the immediate area at first paid only passing attention, but soon the choking stench from the unrelenting sky-clouding plume became too much. After five days, Anne's father Ladislas had had enough and approached the front door of the house with the intention of complaining to the man living there, in the sternest possible way, on behalf of the entire neighborhood. Disappointment and frustration met him instead when he discovered only a note pinned to the door reading: *"Away for one month. Forward mail to 18 Rue des Lombards in Auxerre."* Now worried that perhaps a dangerous chimney fire was raging, one that could easily spread, threatening to engulf nearby homes and businesses, neighbors finally summoned the police. When a pair of officers arrived 21 Rue le Sueur they were told by those living on the street that Dr. Marcel Petiot owned the house, but also had a separate residence a few miles away, referring to the address on the posted note. The two officers looked for a way into the home and finding none, tested the locks on the front door. Secured and sturdy, it was clear they'd need to break down the door to gain entrance. Before taking that drastic measure they instead took a chance and telephoned Dr. Petiot at his other home. After a half-dozen rings Petiot answered. When the police identified themselves and explained their call, Petiot quickly asked if they had entered the house. Informed that they hadn't, he asked the police not to do anything further and that he would be there in 15 minutes. After waiting more than a half hour for Dr. Petiot to arrive, with noxious smoke continuing to pour from the chimney, the policemen had no choice but to call in the fire brigade. Firefighters arrived on scene a short time later, and rather than break down the formidable front door, and seeing no other way into the building on the ground floor, they entered the house through a second story window. Seeking the source of the fire the upper floors were searched first but after finding nothing out of the ordinary the firemen quickly shifted their focus to the basement. There they found the source of the fetid smoke: a coal-burning stove nearly glowing red from the intense, roaring fire inside, and with a charred-black human arm protruding from the open door. Stunned and confused the firefighters then noticed something odd about the pile of coal beside the stove. Mixed into the coal pile were bones and human body parts.

Fascinated and intrigued by what was unfolding below, Anne

observed the entire spectacle from a front room second floor window. She watched as various police and firemen entered the building only to exit a few minutes later, one after another, vomiting and retching in the street below, at first believing they'd been overcome by smoke. With her window opened slightly, she watched as Dr. Petiot finally arrived on the scene and was immediately questioned about the gruesome basement discovery. Petiot made no attempt to hide his guilt, instead he told police he was a member of the French Resistance, and that the bodies were those of German traitors and collaborators. Charming and fully convincing as was his trait, and finding a sympathetic ear for his well rehearsed explanation, police who often looked the other way where resistance fighters and activities were concerned, chose to release Petiot, who promptly vanished. As their investigation of the scene continued police made more grisly discoveries: in the garage to the side of the house they found a large pile of quicklime mixed with human remains, including scalps, skulls and jawbones; in the stable at the back of the house they came across a pit filled with more quicklime and corpses in various stages of decomposition; on a staircase leading from the courtyard to the basement, a canvas sack was found containing the headless and footless left half of a body, its internal organs removed; in another part of the basement investigators discovered large sinks that had been used to drain the blood from corpses plus a hidden soundproof chamber with wall-mounted shackles with a peephole centered in the sturdy door. By the time their investigation ended police attributed 27 known murders to Petiot, although the actual number was most likely much higher. Most of his victims came from an elaborate scheme Petiot had concocted where for the sum of 25,000 francs, he promised safe passage out of France through Portugal and on to Argentina for Jews, resistance fighters or anyone else looking to escape the Nazis and German occupation. Those eager to escape and willing to pay arrived to his home in the middle of the night and were never seen again. Once inside, Petiot would convince his victims that they needed to be inoculated against southern hemisphere diseases before traveling. He would then inject them with lethal drugs, mostly cyanide, and then strip them of all their valuables before dismembering and disposing of their bodies. At first he simply dumped the bodies into the Seine, but word of Petiot's underground escape route spread quickly and before long there were so many people arriving at his door he was forced to devise another method of ridding his house of the mounting number of corpses. By the time the investigation at Petiot's house concluded, the coroner recorded more than 33 pounds of charred bones, 24 pounds of unburned bone fragments, 11 pounds of human hair including at least ten whole scalps, and three full garbage cans of body parts too small to identify.

With the discovery of Petiot's house of death, the scheme behind it, the ongoing manhunt and the public's unquenched morbid fascination, the story quickly escalated into a media frenzy, splashed across the front pages of every paper in France and beyond. Throughout the summer, the search for Paris' serial killer intensified, spurred by headlines dubbing Petiot the "Butcher of Paris", the "Scalper of the Etoile", the "Monster of Rue Le Sueur", the "Demonic Ogre", and "Doctor Satan".

Now however Paris had reason to turn its attention away from the near daily excitement generated by the reliable leads that went nowhere and false Petiot sightings throughout the country that proved equally fruitless. Instead Parisians reveled in their new found freedom after four years of Nazi rule and looked ahead to the next day's celebratory military parade.

For Anne, it also meant her chance to see her brother who she'd not seen since the war began. He'd been living in Guernsey when war broke out and was forced to flee the island ahead of the occupying Germans. Fighting with the French 2nd Armored Division ever since, he had survived and was in Paris, camped with the rest of his unit in the Bois du Boulogne, Paris' second largest park along the western edge of the 16th arrondissement and a short walk from Rue le Sueur.

Anne and her father, along with Anne's school-friend Janine, whose father was head of the police detail in the Bois du Boulogne, were walking near the park when they passed the courtyard of an elegant home facing the park. In the courtyard Recon Troop soldiers who had arrived in Paris ahead of the Division were busy getting fresh water for their canteens and taking the opportunity to clean up after weeks of fighting in the scorching summer heat.

At first Janine thought the handsome, dashing soldier who had been urged on by an elbow from another, equally handsome soldier, was looking at her, but it was in fact Anne that Cletus approached. Under the watchful eye of her father, Cletus introduced himself to Anne, then struggled to remember something, anything, from the impromptu but frequent jeep-side French lessons with Merg. He had been a quick study, even adopting a somewhat convincing accent at times, however at this moment his mind was blank. His face brightened with a wide toothy smile when, after a rapid exchange of French between the girls, followed immediately by nervous laughter, Anne spoke to him in English. His shyness abated, Cletus tried to explain why he and the others were already in Paris ahead of the Division; that the troop had been tasked with reconnoitering and securing the 12 mile route to Paris from the French country palace of Versailles where the Division was currently bivouacked.

Anne then explained why they were heading to the park, telling Cletus about her brave brother, and how much all of Paris would turn out for tomorrow's parade, a parade that she insisted was really in her honor. The look of confusion that struck Cletus brought a spray of laughter to the girls once again. Anne then explained that it was also her 18th birthday tomorrow and so the parade, as she saw it, *should* be in her honor. Cletus laughed along with the girls and reasoned that since it was her birthday, she deserved a birthday kiss that he without hesitation delivered. Anne was wide-eyed with surprise, embarrassment, and fear for she knew the upcoming talk she would later get from her strict and protective father, who suddenly whisked her away from the brash American soldier. For Cletus however, it was a kiss he'd never forget.

Aside from securing the roadways leading from Versailles, another element to the Recon Troop's mission was to establish contact with the French resistance forces, the FFI (*Forces Françaises de l'Intérieur*) to ascertain the location and strength of any remaining German forces. That part of their mission came shortly after arriving on the outskirts of Paris when a car-full of FFI pulled up in front of their vehicles. The leader of the group, a thin man with a thick wave of sweat slicked black hair who looked to be in his late twenties, wearing gold framed round glasses and a two-day splotchy growth of beard, sprang from the car, a captured German machine pistol that American soldiers nicknamed a "burp gun" slung over his shoulder. He tried his best to weave what little English he knew into a coherent message until Merg, standing near the command vehicle with Captain Meisenhelter, came to his rescue. The man whose name was Tristen told them of a group of German soldiers from a quartermaster company whose commander, fearing reprisals from the FFI, had refused to surrender to anyone but the American army. One of the conditions of the surrender however was that someone from the Recon Troop would have to volunteer to be a hostage while the negotiated surrender was conducted, thus ensuring the safety of the German soldiers.

Without hesitation Merg volunteered for the duty. With his fluency in German and French he was also the obvious choice. Merg was taken to an area of the Paris suburbs, to a side street where a crudely constructed barricade blocked access to a main thoroughfare, one that terminated in a cul-de-sac at one end, rimmed with what appeared to be government buildings that had been used by German occupiers for conducting official business. The other end of the avenue continued on into the heart of the city.

The FFI pointed out the location of the waiting Germans around the corner from the blocked street, a white patch of cloth tied to a wooden post marking their location in a building entranceway in the cul-de-sac. Merg climbed the barricade, reminded the FFI not to follow, turned the corner and walked slowly, arms raised to show he had no weapons, approaching what he expected to be frightened, anxious German soldiers. Within earshot he called out to the commander in German, hoping that speaking to them in their native tongue would ease their fears. He was right. A brief conversation ensued, with Merg offering cigarettes and chocolate to the German soldiers, both to ease the tension and to prove that he was indeed an American soldier and not an FFI fighter posing as one because who else but a genuine American soldier "would have Lucky Strikes and Hershey bars?" With that the soldiers now surrounding him relaxed with a laugh. He further put them at ease explaining that his family had come from Germany and that was the reason he spoke German and he assured the nervous enemy soldiers that they had nothing to fear since the Recon Troop would accept their surrender and guarantee their safety.

He then detailed how their surrender would be conducted. Meantime, while the Recon Troop waited for the Germans' surrender, the FFI informed them that thanks to their presence alone, four Army Air Corps pilots and a tail-gunner, who had survived being shot down over France a few weeks earlier and were in hiding in a small town nearby, had finally been freed. A short time later the German soldiers with their arms raised, carrying their weapons above their heads, came walking down the street, with Merg leading them. The FFI watched in surprise as Merg confidently escorted the Germans past the barricaded street and down the avenue, not according to the plans as the FFI had been told. They believed the Germans would be brought to the barricade where one by one the soldiers would be disarmed and searched by the FFI in what was to be their moment of superiority over the Germans who had held their city captive for more than four years. Only then would the Germans, sufficiently humiliated, be allowed to surrender to the Americans. With emotions, tension and tempers elevated in the August heat, Merg, Lt. Hughes and Capt. Meisenhelter believed following the FFI's plan would be a lit fuse on a powder keg and came up with an alternative.

The FFI scrambled over their makeshift barricade, trotted to the end of the side street and could only watch as the group of defeated Germans marched down the middle of the street towards the rumbling engines of the Recon Troop's waiting M-8s and jeeps. General Davis, who had been informed of their intentions, would formally accept the Germans' surrender the following day.

Camped at Versailles the night before the parade, the 28th Infantry Division boarded canvas covered transport trucks on the morning of August 29th and drove through a rainstorm to the Bois de Boulogne. Once there they were ordered to shine their boots, clean their uniforms, trucks, jeeps, tanks, artillery pieces and wash and shave in preparation for the victory march. As the sun began to chase away the morning clouds, the entire division, 15,000 men, marched up the *Avenue Hoche* to the Arc de Triomphe. Suddenly a whistle blew and the 56-piece Keystone marching band began to play "Khaki Bill" to start the parade. Leading the march, jeeps carrying the Division Commander and General Staff rolled through the famous arch followed by the M-8s and jeeps of the 28th Cavalry Recon Troop. Next came the soldiers of the 110th and 112th Regiments, parading side by side in battalion formations of twelve men across, forming an awe-inspiring wall of men marching in unison 24 abreast. Jubilant, frenzied crowds lining the avenue waved flags. They tossed flowers at the soldiers and handed them bottles of wine; kisses and hugs were plentiful. Behind the formidable mass of soldiers came the tank destroyer units, anti-aircraft batteries, field artillery pieces, chemical engineers and medical units that followed in formation. Infantry soldiers from the 109th Regiment came next then additional artillery, armor and tank destroyer units in columns of four. By all standards it was an impressive and prideful display of military might.

The 28th Infantry Division marching down the Champs-Élysées in Paris, August 29, 1944

Photo: National Archives

Anne however missed the grand spectacle. Her father refused to let her go to the parade telling her, "If you think you can just throw yourself into the arms of any American soldier, you've got another thing coming". Anne's argument that it was the American soldier that kissed her and not the other way around fell on Ladislas' deaf ears. Although Cletus never got to see Anne at the parade, he did manage to find Janine and traded chocolate bars for Anne's address. Throughout his time in France and beyond, Cletus would write to Anne regularly.

While Gen. De Gaulle wanted the parade to celebrate the liberation of Paris, Gen. Eisenhower's plans called for bypassing the city completely. However, knowing that de Gaulle's entrance into the city by no means secured it, and fearing Paris could decay into a civil war between those loyal to de Gaulle and communists looking to seize power, Eisenhower instead decided to use the parade to both show cohesive Allied authority and as a practical means of moving the entire division through the city rather than going around it. Eisenhower would write after the war:

> "*it became possibly the only instance in history of troops marching in parade through the capital of a great country to participate in pitched battle on the same day.*"

While a few infantry soldiers and the Recon Troop enjoyed the varied hospitality of the French throughout Paris that afternoon, the rest of the division marched about six miles northeast of Paris to Le Bourget Field, the same airfield where Charles Lindbergh landed his famous "Spirit Of St. Louis" plane after his history making transatlantic flight in 1927. The exuberance of Lindbergh's French welcome the night he landed was now rivaled by the greeting the infantrymen received as they marched to and eventually into the field. Everywhere people handed out bottles of wine, champagne, cognac and whiskey. Cheeses, breads and apples kept appearing while the GIs were showered with flowers, kisses, hugs and anything else that showed French appreciation for their freedom. For the 28th Infantry Division however, the celebrations of that day would be short lived.

The following morning the entire division was sent into battle northeast of Paris, chasing the fleeing Germans across France. The division was met by only pockets of German resistance at first as they pushed on towards the Forest of Compiegne, where the fighting intensified before the 28th seized the heavily defended high ground along the Aisne River. This ground allowed access to the strategically important bridges across the river. A month earlier the 28th was bogged-down in the bloated, rancid, animal corpse strewn, French hedgerow countryside, gaining hard fought ground, yards at a time. Now the Americans, rapidly advancing towards the Belgian border, took the fight to the Germans, gaining miles of territory with each push eastward.

As September dawned, towns or what was left of towns that had suffered pummeling by mortar and artillery, as well as aerial bombardment when the weather allowed, fell in rapid succession. The Keystone division was now racing through the French countryside, along secured highways, advancing an average of 17 miles a day. The rapid advance, while a welcomed surprise to Allied command, now meant reconsidering battle plans once meant for meeting strong German defenses. Instead, reengineered plans now concentrated on keeping a pursuing army supplied with food, ammunition and gasoline. This also helped Allied troops maintain pressure on the retreating German army.

The steady and sweeping divisional gains were due in no small measure to advance intelligence provided by the varied missions of the 28th Cavalry Recon Troop. Working on point and well ahead of the regimental spearheads, the Recon Troop entered into enemy territory to gather intelligence on German installations, troop strengths, movements and most importantly to the present action, to find intact or nearly so, bridges or bridgeheads the Germans had not destroyed which would allow divisional regiments to cross the Meuse river in

France.

Progress however was hampered by the lack of gasoline. The entire division had outrun its supply chain and fuel was at a premium; combined with numerous machine gun covered road blocks set up by the enemy the Wehrmacht rear guard slowed the Recon Troop's reconnaissance efforts and the Division's advance.

With the information obtained through eyes-on reconnaissance, and from captured German documents and maps that Merg could translate on the spot, information moved rapidly through the chain of command, allowing battle plans to be altered and maps quickly redrawn. Merg's skills gave the Recon Troop an immediate on-site battlefield advantage. The Recon Troop could, and often did ,reassess mission specifics gaining information from translated military documents or by talking to civilians and interrogating captured German soldiers.

More often, based on battlefield intelligence, the Recon Troop radioed to divisional command, the map coordinates of suspected camouflaged German fortifications and defenses. The artillery acted quickly redirecting fire, with the Recon Troop acting as forward observers.

Often additional prisoners were taken, with Merg once again gathering scraps of information before sending them back to the divisional CP for further interrogation and processing. The Recon Troop would then hold the town until support troops could arrive, and then they were off to resume their assigned mission.

Resupplied, refueled and with fresh information on the enemy and with the combat engineers busy repairing bridges or building temporary ones, the 28th division was again on the attack. By the middle of the first week in September, the infantry was beginning their push across the border into Belgium, something the Recon Troop had done a day earlier.

NINE

Mario Van Montfort was a well known architect from Brussels when the Germans invaded Belgium in 1940. Believing that his 28-year-old and only son would be forcibly conscripted into the Wehrmacht, Mario convinced him to study in Switzerland while Mario, fearing that the Nazis now in administrative control of the country, might press him into service to the party at best or be persecuted as an intellectual at worst, chose to flee his home with his wife Maria. Together they traveled to the southern Belgium countryside to stay with relatives, living the quite life of a farmer for what he hoped would be short stay.

Four years later and their entire country soon to be liberated, the Van Monforts were preparing for their return to Brussels when on the morning of September 8th the 28th Cavalry Reconnaissance Troop rolled into Chiny, a small town pressed into a horse-shoe bend in the Semois River just north of Sedan in southern Belgium and the closest town to the farm where the Van Montforts had been living. The men of the Recon Troop were immediately struck by the fact that, unlike the town of Florenville a short distant away to the southwest that they had reconnoitered a day earlier for possible use as the divisional CP, most of the buildings of Chiny were intact, showing only modest scars of war.

With the Americans rapidly advancing the Germans chose to fall back rather than waste valuable time and resources fighting to hold the town that had no strategic value. The Recon Troop, liberators once again, were showered with flowers and fruit, about all the people had left to offer after the Germans stripped Chiny of anything they considered valuable.

Merg rode in back of the command jeep as was typical, his constant backseat companion a Browning .50 caliber machine gun. Capt. Lewis Meisenhelter sat in front in the passenger seat with Cletus behind the wheel. They pulled to the side of the main road to allow the other vehicles to take up defensive positions and as always be on the look-out for snipers. Merg immediately struck up conversations in French with several townspeople. He introduced himself and his jeep companions then gathered as much information as possible about German activity in the town. The Van Montforts and the rest of the people in town were happy to offer any information they thought would prove useful in helping their American liberators chase the Germans from their homeland. Perhaps, if for no other reason than he reminded them of the son that they hadn't seen since the Germans came to power, the Van Montforts took an immediate liking to George, who along with the rest of the troop, was sunburned and dirt-covered.

From Mario, George learned that the Germans had hastily retreated from Chiny and presumably the entire river valley in the predawn hours the day before. That news was quickly radioed back to divisional command and the Recon Troop immediately received new orders: to reconnoiter an area to the south of Chiny known as the Charmois region, a picturesque river valley gently winding through the forested countryside on the way to Arlon. Before accepting what the Recon Troop was reporting was true, that the Germans had retreated from the entire valley, divisional command wanted "eyes on" verification.

In Chiny for less than an hour, the troop was once again rolling, and despite running into a few hastily constructed but well defended roadblocks, there was little else in the way of enemy activity. Approaching a couple of the roadblocks, the Recon Troop was forced to engage the enemy when the Germans opened up with mortars and machine guns. What surprised Merg and the others wasn't that the Germans were putting up a fight, an obvious delaying tactic to give the bulk of the German army ample time to fall back, but rather *when* they opened fire on the approaching Recon Troop. At first they thought they were lucky with the Germans having fired upon them well before reaching the road blocks, giving away what would have been their devastating ambush positions.

When the M-8s countered with their cannons and jeep mounted mortars and machine guns, the Recon Troop quickly discovered that the German soldiers left behind to cover the Wehrmacht retreat had no stomach for continuing the fight. Most retreated rather than engaged and simply surrendered the moment the Recon Troop returned fire and were eager to answer Merg's queries and told him that the way south to Arlon would be mostly clear because the Wehrmacht was hastily falling back through Luxembourg and then into Germany. The prisoners were sent back to Chiny with several Recon Troop guards while the remainder of the Recon Troop cautiously pressed on to Arlon, knowing that the information gleaned from the German prisoners may have been purposely misleading or inaccurate as some rear guard soldiers were given false information on overall troop movements in anticipation of their capture.

German intelligence officers hoped that if captured, these soldiers should they answer questions when interrogated, would tell their captors what they knew, thereby seeding the false intelligence up the chain of command. As it turned out, the information given by the German POWs were correct. Because of the rapid advance of the entire division and the Recon Troop, the spearhead of the allied advance was coming into contact with only pockets of German resistance or rear guard soldiers tasked with holding back the allied advance at the crudely constructed road blocks. Regardless, the firefights with these remaining troops were short lived with the Germans retreating, surrendering or dying for the Fatherland. Remarkably the Recon Troop survived these skirmishes with only one soldier wounded in the leg by a piece of shrapnel from a German mortar.

After fighting through the various roadblocks, the Recon Troop crested a hill on the tree lined road carving through the Belgian countryside. Before them; in the distance, a crown of church spires amongst the fertile forest pines, sat Arlon, a municipality dating back to the middle ages and capital of the province of Luxembourg in southeastern Belgium.

The Recon Troop cautiously rolled into town, navigating the spiral of cobblestone streets leading to the town center. As was the case that morning, the streets were soon teaming with people overjoyed by the arrival of their American liberators; their presence coming just hours after the Germans had pulled out of the region. For most of the townspeople it was the first time they'd seen a jeep and soon the Recon Troop could go no further, their progress halted by townspeople wanting to celebrate with the Americans but also wanting a closer look at this wondrous vehicle.

Soon bottles of wine, beer and brandy appeared and were passed amongst the soldiers. Merg stayed to task and tried to get information on the Germans from anyone who would lend an ear. As he spoke in French he was mobbed by townspeople eager to communicate. A man worked his way through the joyous throng to the command jeep and announced that he was a member of the resistance and that he would provide any information he could about German activity, adding that they should not trust the mayor of the town who had, according to this resistance fighter, had been a German collaborator. The information was radioed back to Divisional command and shortly after a platoon of MPs assigned to the Division arrived in town, followed by infantry soldiers. The Recon Troop then received orders to stand down until further notice and return to Chiny.

Arriving back to Chiny by late afternoon, the troop set up camp outside of town in the "Bois du Hat", a forested area on the outskirts of Chiny on the road to Florenville. As George and Cletus were settling into camp George looked up and was surprised to see Mario Van Monfort and his wife standing on the road just beyond where the troop was camped. A quick conversation followed where George asked the Van Monforts if they had any wine "to drink with the Captain".

Without hesitation Van Monfort grabbed George and Cletus and led them to Les Comptes de Chiny, an upscale hotel overlooking the river. There, Van Monfort happily produced several bottles of wine that had been stashed from the Germans. It was also a chance for George and Cletus to wash up with hot water and real soap after nearly five hot summer weeks.

Cleaned and shaved, they brought the bottles of wine back to share with the rest of the HQ platoon and then went to the Van Monfort home, where they had been invited for dinner. Although Cletus could understand and speak some French, George was more than happy to translate on his friend's behalf. The following day, while the Recon Troop remained in stand down mode, George, Cletus, Charles Stansbury, Joe Vocasek and Pvt. George Raduykovich returned to the Van Monfort home where, over afternoon tea, each talked about their home. Generous, kind and eager to know more about the soldiers' lives, and reminding him of his parents, George had grown fond of the Van Monforts in the short time he'd come to know them. George told the Van Monforts about his home in Rye, NY on the outskirts of New York City and what it was like to grow up there. He shared details about his days at Princeton and showed them photographs of his parents. He also shared the latest editions of magazines his mother had sent, including "The National Geographic" and "Vogue", the latter featuring the latest fashion trends in hats and furs and also providing a pictorial array of bomb-scarred London. The pictures were taken by

Lee Miller, who had already made her mark as a preeminent photo-journalist of the war. For the soldiers the afternoon passed much too quickly. Before they left, they all exchanged addresses and promised to get in touch once the war was over.

The next morning the Recon Troop was preparing to move out. As they broke camp the Van Monforts arrived to say goodbye. Hugs were exchanged and George presented Mrs. Van Monfort with his copies of the magazines they had looked through the night before. George promised to contact them once the war ended and invited them to visit New York where they could meet his parents and where he would happily be their tour guide. Soon the Recon Troop was on the road again heading northeast as part of Division Task Force X, its mission to provide protection to the southern flank of the division, an assignment that would take them into Luxembourg, where on September 10th, it joined with American forces that entered into Luxembourg City after the Germans once again chose to retreat without a fight. After nearly five years of Nazi occupation, Luxembourg celebrated its liberation.

With Luxembourg liberated, the Recon Troop moved swiftly, journeying up to the Siegfried Line, Germany's western fortifications stretching nearly 400 miles and comprised of more than 18,000 pillboxes, bunkers and tank traps. Throughout the rest of September the Recon Troop hovered in this region, acting as a buffer between the 28th Infantry Division to the north and the Third Armor Division to the south. There they patrolled a 25-mile stretch of the Siegfried Line along the Our River, the border between Luxembourg and Germany and part of the border between Belgium and Germany. Soldiers of the Recon Troop manned forward observation posts along this tract as well as making reconnaissance runs along "Skyline Drive", a stretch of paved road paralleling the Our River valley overlooking Germany to the east and the Clerf River valley and Luxembourg to the west.

Aside from the occasional volley of artillery shells fired at the forward observation posts, or the few skirmishes across the river with

German patrols, or the infrequent night reconnaissance, there was little action to be had during this time. The Recon Troop finally enjoyed some R&R (rest and relaxation) in and around the town of Clervaux. Between patrols and duty assignments, the soldiers had a chance to stroll the cobbled stone streets of the town, explore the centuries old castle that loomed over the place, and enjoy hot food and warm beer or wine served in the numerous restaurants.

After more than two weeks of rolling patrols up and down Skyline drive, the Recon Troop was ordered to an area north east of Malmedy, Belgium, known as Camp Elsenborn. Established as a military camp before the turn of the century after the Prussian wars, it initially accommodated more than 4000 cavalry and infantry soldiers and horses that would train under live artillery fire exercises. During the First World War, while under British control, the camp was expanded to house even more troops, readying them for front line battle conditions. The expanded role of the camp also proved a boon to the economy of surrounding towns that saw local laborers employed in the construction of various camp buildings, raw building materials supplied by local factories, food supplies provided by area farms and towns awash with soldiers spending army pay in restaurants and taverns. However the end of the war in 1918 saw the number of troops housed at Camp Elsenborn steadily dwindle, and when the British finally abandoned the camp, the Belgian government assumed control, using it for basic training of the Belgian army. It was in the spring of 1940, when the Germans swept through and occupied Belgium and the Low Countries, that they began using the camp as training ground for the Wehrmacht. Now four years later, the camp was in the hands of the American Army, who now used Camp Elsenborn primarily as a staging area for the eventual and possibly final push into Germany.

For the Recon Troop Camp Elsenborn would be their home for most of October while their official assignment had them maintaining contact between the 109th infantry regiment and the 102nd cavalry group that were protecting the division's left flank. Both were deployed in defensive positions along a 20 mile stretch of the Siegfried Line. Although manning forward observation posts, running jeep patrols or acting as messengers, overall this proved to be easy duty for the Recon Troop, as there were no enemy engagements whatsoever. Considering the extended break in the fighting, it was understandable that hopes ran high that the war would be over by Christmas. The Germans had all but withdrawn into their homeland and were no doubt preparing for a full on defense of that land, while allied troops for the most part held their positions, allowing front line troops to be resupplied and reinforced.

For the next few weeks the men of the Recon Troop enjoyed well deserved downtime while replacement soldiers joined their ranks and the troop saw the arrival of what turned out to be much needed foul weather gear. Seemingly overnight the weather changed markedly as winter's harsh hand began reaching deeper into the low countries. Gray, overcast skies lingered over the valley while temperatures unexpectedly plummeted. Cold rain and light snow fought frequently for ascendency. Fields became ice-crusted bogs while unpaved roads thickened with mud by the unusually early arrival of harsh winter weather. As the end of October neared, the Recon Troop along with the rest of the 28th Infantry Division was on the move again, this time heading northeast to a fifty square mile patch of thickly forested land just across the German-Belgian border called the Huertgen Forest.

Meanwhile in Paris, the end of October would also bring an end to the manhunt for a now notorious serial killer.

TEN

Henri Valéri, a captain with the French Forces of the Interior (FFI) was easily recognized by his neatly groomed full mustache and beard and well known for his charm, wit and intellect. He was also admired for his efficiency in the hunting and purging of Nazi collaborators following the liberation of Paris back in August. His zeal and relentlessness earned him a reputation for tenaciousness and made him the ideal choice to head the FFI's counterespionage and interrogation unit in the 12th arrondissement, known as the Reuilly district ,located on the right bank of the Seine River in the southeast section of Paris. However, soon after assuming that role, some officers under his command became dubious of his judgment as a leader when in September of 1944, two FFI soldiers in his ranks killed the elderly mayor of the town of Tessancourt, who they insisted was a Nazi collaborator, although there was never any proof to back their claim. In truth, the pair was attempting to cover the fact that they'd also robbed him of 12.5 million francs and a valuable stamp collection. What the men didn't know was that the mayor's murder was witnessed by three youths who immediately reported the crime to Capt. Valéri. Outraged by their accusation against his men, Valéri responded by charging the boys with making false statements against his men and tossed them into jail. When an FFI lieutenant who thought Valéri acted irrationally in jailing the boys attempted to look deeper into the case, Valéri ordered him off the investigation, declaring that he would look into the matter personally. After his brief investigation into the matter, Valéri did release the three boys and also summoned the two FFI soldiers for further questioning. Following a short interrogation of the duo Valéri, satisfied with their recounting of events, released the FFI soldiers. They then promptly vanished without a trace, along with the money from the robbery.

A few days following the murder and robbery of the mayor of Tessancourt, an article appeared in the newspaper "Résistance" with a headline accusing the fugitive Dr. Marcel Petiot of being a "soldier of the Reich". The article went on to to claim, among other sordid deeds, that in March of 1943 Petiot had worn a German uniform while hunting down French resistance fighters near Avignon on behalf of the Gestapo. The article infuriated Petiot, who remained in hiding and, through an attorney he'd worked with years earlier, he wrote a letter in response condemning the article as a collection of "filthy Kraut lies that it takes about two grains of good French common sense to see through". Petiot was right. The article was a lie; a ruse meant to flush out the mass murderer who had managed to elude police throughout the summer thanks to the help of sympathetic patients and friends who believed his claims of innocence, having convinced them that the bodies found in the house were those of Germans or Nazi collaborators. Petiot's quick response to the article as well as certain elements in his letter convinced authorities that he was still in France, most likely still in Paris and quite possibly hiding within the ranks of the FFI. The hunt for Petiot intensified anew.

Although his judgments and actions in the Tessancourt incident may have cast a shadow over his command, FFI leaders knew the dogged Capt. Valéri, together with other high ranking FFI officers, offered them the best chance of finding and capturing Petoit, and enlisted them to help with the search effort that was now concentrated in and around the Reuilly district. While police and military security began the laborious task of comparing handwriting samples from Petiot's letter with those of the thousands of FFI officers and fighters, Capt. Valéri and the others ran constant patrols searching bars, restaurants and public places throughout the area. They were also instructed to be mindful of those within the FFI ranks as there was now the high likelihood that Petiot was masquerading as one of their soldiers.

On the morning of October 31, the search for Petiot finally ended. Acting on new information about a possible sighting, Capt. Valéri entered a metro station on the east edge of Paris. He descended the steps and made his way to the platform where a military officer Valéri recognized approached and asked for the time. Valéri paused and pushed up his coat sleeve to look at his watch. Instantly the officer deftly slapped handcuffs onto Valéri's wrist. Confusion registered across Valéri's face that a split-second later was contorted by a grimace of pain when the officer landed a powerful kick into the Captain's stomach knocking the air out of his lungs. The officer spun, forcing Valéri to the ground. From out of the shadows of the metro platform, three other men ran in, jumped on Valéri and pinned him down, quickly binding his feet. The four men then hoisted Valéri up and carried him up the steps to a waiting car outside the metro stop. The seven-month manhunt for Dr. Marcel Petiot, hiding in the guise of FFI Captain Henri Valéri, was finally over. Following the war, Petiot was tried for his crimes and found guilty on 26 counts of murder. On May 25, 1946 at 5:05am, the guillotine dropped on the Butcher of Paris.

While Petiot was being hauled away after capture on that cool October morning, the men of the 28th Cavalry Reconnaissance Troop along with the rest of the 28th Infantry Division were holding their positions in and around the town of Germeter, Germany preparing to launch an attack into the Huertgen Forest. Part of Germany's "Western Wall", the forest was actually comprised of three separate forests and taking it was considered a vital objective and part of the overall battle plan for the push to Berlin. Securing the Huertgen would shore up the right flank of the massive Allied push eastward to the Rhine. Plus, due to the size, denseness and location of the Huertgen, only a dozen miles east of the Belgian border, Allied command believed the Huertgen afforded the Germans what could be an ideal staging area to consolidate troops for a counteroffensive. An additional objective was taking control of several dams controlling the flow of the Roer River. Allied command believed the Germans, in a desperate attempt to defend their homeland, would destroy the dams, thereby flooding the river valley, thus delaying the Allied advance deeper onto German soil. What awaited attacking American troops however was like nothing they had encountered thus far and was beyond anything they could have imagined.

Densely packed clusters of ages-old pines and hardwoods stretching skyward sometimes a hundred feet or more made the Grimm-like forest a dark and foreboding place with treetops weaving a canopy that eclipsed the sun even on the brightest days and from where water seemed to constantly drip even on those rare days when it wasn't raining or at this time of year snowing. Natural obstacles of steep, slippery, wooded ravines plunged to a forest floor festooned with decades old fallen trees and thick branches where decaying twigs, leaves and ferns mixed with mud and mold that produced a suffocating stench. The banks of the many rain-swollen streams veining through the forest were thickened by wild undergrowth, while the few narrow logging roads snaking through the Huertgen were clogged with thick, calf-deep mud the product of four weeks of near continuous rain and snow. Relentless cloud cover kept Army Air Corps planes grounded, while narrow, twisting, mud-clogged forest roads rendered armor support useless, relegating them to the towns and open expanses bordering the thick of the forest. The fight for the Huertgen would come down solely to the infantry soldier.

As part of the Siegfried Line and its western most defenses,

Germany began preparing the Huertgen for a homeland defense in 1938. Every part of the forest had been pre-sighted for mortar and artillery fire, while along the high ridges that weaved throughout the forest concrete pillboxes, log covered dugouts, machine-gun and mortar placements were constructed at short intervals so that no part of the forest couldn't be covered by defending fire. Thousands of mines of various types, including those made of wood that couldn't be detected by mine detection equipment, were seeded in the rare areas of open ground and along the logging roads and trails, the latter mined to such a degree that anti-personnel mines were buried in a staggered pattern every eight or nine paces. Along the ravines below the pillboxes and machine gun nests, barbed wire was spooled out in double crossing rows for hundreds of yards, while in certain areas trees and undergrowth were kept meticulously pruned to allow for a greater field of crossing fire in expected kill zones for uphill attacking enemy troops.

American soldiers in the Huertgen Forest, November 1944

Photo: National Archives

It was the 9th Infantry Division that first encountered the "hell of the Huertgen", as some soldiers had come to refer to it, while others called it the "Green Valley of Death". Fighting there since mid-September, they managed to take and hold the town of Germeter, but despite desperate and exhausting battles eastward that saw towns and tracts of land change hands between German and American troops several times, the 9th Infantry Division was unable to advance much further while taking heavy losses. By the time the remaining exhausted, filthy and in many cases "shell-shocked" soldiers were rotated out of the Huertgen at end of October, the 9th had sustained more than 4500 battlefield casualties. Despite the staggering losses under these horrific conditions and frontline reports detailing the extent and strength of the German defenses, Allied command insisted on continuing the infantry attack by committing fresh divisions to the fight.

After long driving rains the decision was made to delay the attack until the extreme weather eased even slightly, in hopes that planned air support could be utilized. After two days of waiting and with what seemed no end to the horrid weather in sight, the decision to commence the attack came on November 2, 1944. Following a punishing hour-long artillery barrage that saw more than 11,000 rounds fired at German positions along the entire front, three regiments of the 28th attacked south and eastward with the main objective being the taking of the high ground, crossroads town of Schmidt at the southern edge of the Huertgen.

Under a barrage of returning artillery fire, the 109th regiment swung sharply east, attacking on the division's left flank through dense woods to take areas around the town of Huertgen. According to the overall battle plan, the 109th would act as a protective buffer should the Germans try mounting a counter-attack southwest through the woods toward the town of Vossenack, a maneuver they executed successfully against the 9th Infantry Division the week before. The taking of

Vossenack, and more importantly the Vossenack ridge overlooking a steep wooded gorge that plunged to the swift-flowing Kall River below, fell to elements of the 112th regiment, while battalions of the110th regiment attempted to push south on the division's right flank with their initial objective being to secure the Strauch-Schmidt road, thereby opening a key supply route to Schmidt for a later phase of the attack. The main thrust of the assault on Schmidt would fall to the 112th regiment.

Their reconnaissance vehicles also rendered ineffective by winding, mud-laden and dangerously mined logging roads, the 28th Cavalry Recon Troop took up defensive positions on high ground just south of the town of Jägerhaus, on the 110th regiment's right flank. Positioned in a divisional observation outpost overlooking the Kall River, a nearby dam and the battalion of Germans defending it, and the formidable German defenses on the other side of the river, the Recon Troop was able to help direct fire for artillery units while protecting the 110th regiment's southern shoulder should the Germans attempt to swing around and counter-attack from the south. The Recon Troop also closely monitored enemy troop movements and activity at the dam and immediately reported any movement and direction of those troops back to headquarters; the information was then passed onto G-2, the army's intelligence sector. Additionally the Recon Troop was tasked with maintaining a steady flow of communication between the 110th regiment to their east and the 102nd Cavalry Squadron in control of an area well west of the main battle plan around the town of Lammersdorf. The Recon troop also maintained regular foot patrols to reconnoiter and evaluate enemy movements and positions along the north-south road running along the Kall River and on unmarked trails throughout the area that were not visible on aerial reconnaissance photos. This, as it turned out, became vital to the main effort of the 110th regiment's drive southward. Using these previously unknown trails, units from the 110th were able to gain a foothold while attempting to move down the densely treed slopes to a main road leading south toward Rollesbroich. Only then did they hit a solid wall of enemy resistance aided by the dozen or so well placed pillboxes astride the road in what became known as the Raffelsbrand strong point.

For Merg and the rest of the Recon Troop, the routine foot patrols proved to be the most dangerous missions, despite the lack of any direct contact with enemy troops. While the rest of the division was slugging it out in the heart of the forest, with fog, mist, rain and the dense forest growth cutting visibility down to only a dozen yards or so in any direction, and taking heavy losses as a result, the soldiers of the Recon Troop were under near constant mortar and artillery fire. So intense was the shelling that at times the soldiers couldn't tell if it was German or American artillery raining down. Both the Recon Troop soldiers and infantrymen soon learned that during an artillery attack the best chance for survival was to plaster their bodies against the trunks of trees rather than dive to the ground for cover as they had been trained to do. Well aware of the forest density, the Germans quickly employed new strategies in their battle to repel the advancing American troops. German artillery units began firing at the tops of the towering trees, the exploding shells showering the area below with deadly white-hot shrapnel as well as splintered limbs and tree branches. In the Huertgen many soldiers were killed or injured when crushed or impaled by falling timber. German mortar teams also honed their skills on GIs hunkered down in foxholes or dugouts by firing a series of shells: one long, the next short, with the last finding its target obliterating the foxhole and the soldiers positioned there. The technique was typical of well known German efficiency and ruthlessness and also had a demoralizing effect on the American troops watching helplessly as the Germans spent shell after shell on one foxhole or dugout until that group soldiers was killed, then redirected their fire to the next target and repeated the tactic. American GIs seeing the progression of the mortar attack and knowing their time was coming, would try to make a run for safety but most were cut down by covering machine gun fire. At night, when the cover of darkness prevented accurate artillery targeting and allowed for rare moments of quiet, weaved with the sound of falling rain that tantalizingly reminded the soldiers of sizzling bacon, came the eerie cries and moans of the wounded and dying lying somewhere in the woods, the medics unable to reach them.

Fighting in the Huertgen also meant battling near epidemic trench-foot, a condition caused by exposing the feet to prolonged damp and cold conditions combined with poor hygiene, all of which were in full flourish in the Huertgen. Attempting to keep warm, blood vessels constrict, thereby reducing blood flow to the extremities resulting in tissue and nerve damage. Some soldiers attempted to keep their feet dry by placing socks inside their shirts, hoping body heat would dry them during the day allowing them to change their socks each night. Rampant dysentery and illness brought on by constant cold, exhaustion, mold and no hot food also took their toll on the American troops.

In the Huertgen, humanity itself was often under attack. Weeks of steady, savage fighting, sometimes hand-to-hand and under grueling inhumane conditions, took a toll on both sides: weaponless soldiers, arms raised in surrender, were often shot down rather than taken prisoner, since taking prisoners meant marching them to the rear for interrogation and eventual evacuation, then returning to the battle lines, all the while be exposed to the enemy, especially sniper fire; a GI proudly carrying a canvas bag of teeth with gold fillings, kicked, cut or pried from the mouths of dead Germans he'd come across in the forest; two American soldiers ordered to escort a German POW to the rear had refused the German a drink of water from their canteens, instead pointing him to a nearby stream where, when the German soldier crouched down to drink from the stream, one of the GIs stepped on the German's neck, forcing his head down into the muddy stream-bed while the other held the German's legs, drowning him; the Germans placing mines or explosive charges rigged with trip wires under the bodies of dead or severely wounded American soldiers, set to detonate when their bodies were moved.

Despite these and other horrific occurrences there were times when humanity triumphed. Truces were sometimes called, allowing both sides to treat the wounded with American and German medics often working side-by-side trying to save lives regardless of uniform. Soldiers from both sides joining together to carry litters to waiting ambulances. For some Germans it was the first time they'd seen black soldiers, who were serving in the Huertgen as ambulance drivers in the mostly segregated US Army of the time.

After more than two weeks of deadly fighting in the Huertgen, the 28th Infantry Division by way of the 112th regiment was able to take and hold the town of Vossenack. They were also able to achieve their primary objective of taking the town of Schmidt albeit briefly. Continued cloud cover grounded planned air support meant to neutralize German Panzer units that, when rolled into action, would force the 112th to withdraw from the town. The 109th regiment managed to take and hold territory to the east of Vossenack, with some battalions then sent to reinforce the 112th.Meanwhile 110th regiment made virtually no gain in their attack southward toward their primary objective of securing the Strauch-Schmidt supply route while taking enormous casualties. By the time the 28th division was rotated out of the fighting in mid-November, two-thirds of the division, some 6000 men, were killed, wounded, missing, captured, or suffering from non-battle maladies. Some of those casualties were replacement soldiers who arrived into the Huertgen as the battle raged and some of them were killed or wounded within hours after arriving, prompting Ernest Hemingway, who at that time was a war correspondent for Collier's Magazine, to quip that it would "save everybody a lot of trouble if they just shot them as soon as they got out of the trucks." *

Relieved from the Huertgen the 28th Infantry Division was sent west to the rear, well away from any front line action to what was known as the quiet sector in Luxembourg. The 28th Cavalry Recon Troop also headed to Luxembourg, to a small town north of the divisional headquarters in Wiltz. A town called Eschweiler.

---

*   *The heaviest fighting in the Huertgen Forest occurred in the three months from September to December, 1944. Officially the Huertgen Forest Battle ended in February 1945, making it the longest battle on German soil during World War II, and the single longest running battle in U.S. Army history. More than 24,000 Americans were killed, missing, captured or wounded, plus another 9,000 soldiers suffered from trench foot, respiratory diseases and combat fatigue. German casualties numbered more 28,000.*

ELEVEN

A day after the troop settled into Eschweiler, Joe Vocasek returned from divisional headquarters in Wiltz with a jeep near overflowing with mailbags. He had gone there to drop off all the letters the soldiers had written since arriving into Eschweiler. It also meant collecting all the mail that had piled up while the troop was in fighting in the Huertgen. Although some mail did manage to make it to soldiers desperate to remain connected to the security of home while fighting to stay alive in that hellish valley, getting and delivering mail exposed Vocasek and whomever accompanied him to needless danger and therefore the trips back to divisional command were severely limited.

As soon as he arrived into town Vocasek's jeep was quickly set upon by the Recon Troop eager for word from home. He deftly doled out the batches of letter and parcels, making sure he bellowed the name Mergenthaler even though George was standing only a few steps away, eliciting laughs from the other soldiers. Vocasek then handed Merg the numerous packages bearing the post mark and return address of the Commodore Hotel. As expected, Merg immediately chose to share the newly arrived bounty, however this time and for the remainder of their time in Eschweiler, the tinned cakes, cookies and candies, including an assortment of Springerle, were divvied up amongst the children of Eschweiler. Smiling faces quickly devoured the soldier's treats that came "all the way from America". It was because of whatever came in those frequently arriving tins plus items George was able to procure from army supplies or from the several trips he made to Clervaux, that he quickly became known for his unwavering generosity to the townspeople and in particular the children. It was certainly that generosity and kindness that in part caught the eye of Virginia Huberty.

Thirty two years old and the youngest of seven children, and despite the younger girls living next door, Virginia drew more than her share of unwanted attention from soldiers from both sides during this uncertain and precarious time of war. As a result she did what she could to tamp down her attractiveness. Her long flowing curls of chestnut hair were kept tucked up under one of her older brother's old caps that she wore everyday while working the farm. Well worn men's pants, though somewhat tailored for her small frame, were still absurdly big, gathered in belted bunches around her waist, the long pant cuffs rolled up and held in place with a stitch. One of her brother's old, farm soiled shirts billowed out from beneath the coverall that draped her slender frame. Mud and field encrusted boots completed an outfit that was her standard daily dress during the nearly five years of German occupation. With the American soldiers now in her town and in her house, she'd have happily continued her masquerade until war's end had it not been for that one young, selfless, German speaking American soldier, the one with the soft welcoming eyes and engaging smile, the one all the girls in town took an immediate interest in. Not long after she first spied George however Virginia moved the few dresses she had to the front of the wardrobe and let her brother's old cap rest on a peg by the door.

For George there was something about the girl in the baggy clothes that immediately struck him. She was older than he but didn't look it and her youthful vigor and passion for life were infectious. George saw past the frump and instead saw a young woman trying overly hard to look unapproachable and despite her best intentions, as far as he was concerned, failing magnificently. He guessed at the reason for her disheveled appearance and for George that made her even more attractive. He saw past her stained working clothes and at times off-putting behavior, seeing instead her soft face, bared of makeup, her full lips, high-arching cheeks reddened from sun and cool autumn wind, her light brown eyes bright and alluring, possessing a certain radiance that made them easy to get lost in and difficult to return from.

More and more, George's off duty down time seldom translated into rest time, choosing instead to work at whatever needed tending to on the various farms around Eschweiler. Carrying hay to the animals or bringing buckets of water to fill troughs, cleaning out stalls or chopping and stacking wood, were just ways of trying to be as close to Virginia as possible and spending as much time with her as times would allow. When they weren't working the farm the two would take frequent walks together or sit beside the fire in the Huberty house talking for hours. Often, when George wasn't having dinner in the parsonage with Cletus and Father Bodson, he shared dinner with either the Huberty or Pletschet family, the two nearly interchangeable, bringing army supplied food items to share. Sometimes Cletus joined them, other times it was just George by himself. It was after one of those dinners sitting with Virginia and some of the girls from the Pletschet house that George shared the few photos he had of his parents at their home in Rye, New York: the one of his mother in her wedding dress, his parents in their garden and the color photo of him taken just days before he left for training in Wales, standing in front of Alice's well tended garden, the Christmas roses nearly in bloom. Explaining the roses brought thoughts of the approaching holidays.

The American holiday of Thanksgiving was near, and George and Cletus planned to spend the evening in the parsonage with Father

Bodson, with the priest's cook set to prepare as close to a traditional Thanksgiving meal as could be arranged with most of the ingredients including a turkey, coming from George, the fruits of deals struck and items traded with the company cooks. Wine for the dinner would come from Father Bodson, from bottles hidden away during the German occupation. Explaining the holiday to the girls, its tradition and meaning dovetailed into their mentioning of the holiday for the town that was also approaching: St. Nicolas Day on December 6th.

Preceding the family centric holiday of Christmas by a few weeks, St. Nicolas Day celebrates the patron saint of children and is considered a town-wide celebration. The holiday springs from a centuries-old legend telling of an evil butcher who had killed three children, intending to turn them into sausage, but with God's help St. Nicolas, or the "Kleeschen", as he's known throughout Luxembourg, brought the children back to life then slayed the evil butcher. Through the years the holiday grew and now tradition dictates that St. Nicolas and his helper "Houseker," or Black Peter, enter the houses in town on the night of December 5, the eve of St. Nicolas Day, to bring children presents. Days prior his visit, excited children are told to put their shoes, originally made of wood, on windowsills or by their bedroom doors so that the Kleeschen can leave chocolates, candy, fruits or other sweets and presents in the shoes of good children deserving of presents. The following day, the Kleeschen would arrive into town on a sleigh and grateful children would gather around, anxious to tell St. Nicolas what they hoped for on Christmas. Under Nazi occupation however, St. Nicolas Day was banned as it was not a sanctioned German holiday. Throughout Luxembourg in private, families still marked the day without any public fanfare, and St. Nicolas himself never came to any towns or villages in Luxembourg. Now nearly five years later, throughout Luxembourg, people would finally be able to mark the holiday, however the German occupation had taken a toll on the populace and basic living supplies were scarce; festive treats and presents even more so. Determined to reclaim and reestablish their country and heritage, the girls emphasized that this St. Nicolas Day would be celebrated regardless, even if treats and presents were lacking, "as long as we have a visit from the Kleeschen".

The holiday history lesson absorbed, George now was resolute not to let this St. Nicolas Day pass as something less than it should be. It would be the first to be celebrated throughout the town since war came to Eschweiler, and for some children too young to remember a time without war, growing up only hearing about the holiday but never experiencing it outside of their homes, it would be their first time ever seeing the Kleeschen. George became obsessed with gathering anything he could from his fellow soldiers, anything from their rations or supplies or from care packages from home to donate to the holiday. He also wrote home, explaining the holiday and what it meant to the townspeople and especially the children, asking his parents to urgently send whatever they could immediately gather to help the celebration. As for the long awaited arrival of the Kleeschen, one of the older men from the town, Aline Arend, assumed the role, with Victoria Pletschet playing "black Peter".

With days to spare, George received several large parcels from home containing as much candy, chocolates, cookies and cakes as could be sent as quickly as possible, his father using any and all means at his disposal to ensure the parcels arrived in time. The contents of those parcels, combined with everything collected from the Recon Troop soldiers who were more than happy to give, plus with whatever George and Cletus could buy in Clervaux, would mean that the children of Eschweiler would have a St. Nicolas Day they'd never forget.

When St. Nicolas Day arrived, word had been spread through town that the Kleeschen would be at the Pletschet house by late afternoon. The cold misty rain that had blanketed the town for most of the day, by late afternoon faded leaving only a stiff breeze to accompany children on their way to the Pletschet house. Once there they found the treat-laden Kleeschen waiting for them. For more than an hour children arrived and were given brown paper bags filled to the brim with treats. Hot cocoa was also on offer, courtesy of Hershey bars from soldiers' rations that were melted down by Father Bodson's cook. Smiling children, some of whom had only heard the tale of the Kleeschen but had never actually seen him, were wide eyed with amazement that the Kleeschen, who clearly was real, had finally come to Eschweiler. Before all returned home, Father Bodson led everyone in a prayer on this special day, with special mention given to the Kleeschen's American helpers. Prayers were also given for a swift end to the war and the safe return home for all.

The small St. Nicolas Day party over, George and several members from the Recon Troop and some townspeople, including Virginia and her brother Michel, gathered at the Pletschet farmhouse following the celebration. There George handed out small presents to all gathered; token gifts meant to mark the special occasion. For Michel, a new army issued razor with several packages of replacement blades, a hard to find item anywhere but on the black market these days. For Virginia and the other girls, woolen scarves chosen by George's mother. For the Pletschet family, tins of ground coffee, canned fruits and spam. For his fellow soldiers, magazines, new pens, gloves, knitted wool scarves and hats, tinned cakes, and anything else that arrived in the parcels from home. For Father Bodson, photography a new found hobby prior to the war, a few hard to come by rolls of film for his camera, the takeaway from a deal struck with a signal company photographer a week earlier; wine for film. There was however one package that came with specific instructions: it was to be opened only by George, a present from his mother. In front of the Pletschet and Huberty families and a handful of Recon Troop soldiers George unwrapped his early Christmas present.

"Nice...not exactly OD, but nice," Cletus remarked as George held up the large, plum colored sweater vest. George immediately recognized his mother's handiwork, knitting being one of her favorite pastimes, one she had become quite skillful at over the years as evidenced by the tight weave of this perfectly sized garment. Growing up George clearly remembered staving off many a Rye winter with the help of his mother's hand knitted hats and mittens, with large crocheted blankets smothering every bed in the house assuring warm slumbers. George immediately tossed off his field jacket then pulled the sweater on over his shirt, pulling his shirt collar through the generous neck of the sweater, then tugging at the bottom edge and smoothing his shirt folds beneath. He stood for a few moments enjoying his gift, modeling in a way while memories pooled.

"It's warm, that's for sure," said George noting the weight of the wool trapping his body heat. He threw his field jacket back on and zipped it, showing the other GIs that he'd have no problem wearing it under his jacket. In fact in the days ahead the sweater became a regular part of George's daily dress, always over his army issued shirt and under his jacket. Soon everyone in Eschweiler, civilian or soldier could easily spot George if for no other reason than the striking contrast of the purple sweater peeking out from under his "olive drab" army jacket.

St. Nicolas Day now passed, George and the other soldiers returned to daily life in town. Often Merg was called upon to act as an interpreter or help with translations when townspeople tried bartering, or at the very least, talking to the soldiers living amongst them. So frequent came the requests that one evening in the parsonage, while well wined, George, with input from Cletus and Father Bodson, took the time to jot down on slips of paper some of the most common phrases needed both in English and German, and handed notes to the townspeople and soldiers alike for ready reference.

"How goes it", "It goes well", "There is no whiskey in town" and "Have you any soap for eggs" seemed to be the most frequently used, most useful phrases. George also jotted down the translation for "No, I will not go out with you", meant as a joke to his fellow Recon Troop soldiers, thinking they should be used to hearing that from the girls at the Pletschet and Huberty houses. Overall the crib notes worked, with townspeople sometimes substituting other words for "eggs" such as "bier" considering who they were speaking with. Still there were times when George was pressed into service for more complicated conversations.

Original phrase note written by George Mergenthaler

It was in the parsonage that George felt most at home while in Eschweiler. On evenings, when not with Virginia or posted on guard duty or out on patrol, George could usually be found talking with Father Bodson and often, his acute appetite for reading heightened, George would help himself to a book from the shelves, sometimes reading it in its entirety that evening by the fire. Most mornings George attended early mass with the townspeople and usually assisted Father Bodson with services while at other times he would come into the church to pray or to be alone or sometimes just to read. For George, there was just something about St. Mauritius that he was drawn to. Perhaps it was the intimate, welcoming size of the small church with its ornately carved rich wood accents, or the sturdy wooden altar and the mural behind it depicting Jesus passing loaves of bread to the masses: the bread of life, or maybe it was the way the brass pipes of the organ seemed to tower majestically, rising as if pointing to heaven, or the way the morning light shone through the stained glass windows bathing the interior with a warm, soothing, inviting light or how after arching over the steeple, the afternoon sun would respond in kind through windows on the other side for evening prayers. Perhaps it was all that and something more, not of the church but of himself that despite all he'd seen and done as a soldier with an army fighting an enemy across a continent, that more than anywhere at any time since leaving for war had he been able to find solace, sanctuary or salvation anywhere but here. To George, for reasons he didn't question and couldn't explain, he simply felt at peace in St. Mauritius.

Immediately after attending morning mass, George would join Cletus and quite often Stans in helping the townspeople with chores on the various farms. One morning, before they headed off to the fields or barns, Father Bodson, his hobby interest renewed with his gift of film and seizing the seemingly rare opportunity of clear skies and a bright winter sun, snapped a few photos of George, Stans and Cletus. Beside the church the three posed for pictures that the priest promised he'd make copies of for all three soldiers. Having learned about optimal lighting conditions, the priest posed the three men to take advantage of the morning sun. Pictures taken, the soldiers journeyed off, with George making sure as usual that his self-appointed tasks landed him somewhere within sight of Virginia. Spreading hay for the cows each morning became routine, as did milking, something George learned to do with tutoring and encouragement from Virginia. Although slow to learn he eventually caught on to the correct amount of pressure needed to squeeze the base of the teats between his thumbs and forefingers allowing the milk to flow down. Then as instructed he rolled his remaining fingers down the teats forcing the milk out and into the bucket positioned beneath the utters. His large frame however made squatting on the milking stool almost impossible and despite cautions to the contrary he took to one knee to get the job done.

When not tending to the cows or farm work and chores in general, George could usually be found playing with the children of Eschweiler; sometimes playing in whatever was the game of the moment, other times George would entertain the children with stories of Texas and of New York City, occasionally embellishing insignificant details strictly for the entertainment value to his audience. "Cows as big as houses", "So hot the Devil himself won't go there", "Buildings so tall they sway on the wind", were some of the claims, met with wonderment, with disbelief and with George wide-eyed and smiling, with giggles. Other times he would read to them, something from one of the books borrowed from the priest. Intentionally or not, George quickly became a favorite of the children of Eschweiler; a substitute for the older brother or father they hadn't seen in years.

Reconnaissance duties also kept the troop active during this down time. Reports coming back from people living near the front lines told of steady German activity, although no specifics could be given. People reported hearing constant motorized traffic in the area and often that meant the addition of German troops in the area. From what locals could gather it seemed the Germans were attempting a build up of troops and supplies just over the border. Several Recon patrols were dispatched to verify the claims of the locals. Patrols were mostly done at night under the cover of darkness. Once again the men would blacken their faces and remove all but the most basic uniform pieces so as to create as little noise as possible, considering they would be moving close to if not behind enemy lines. As always the mission was to gather eyes-on intelligence and report their findings back to divisional command and G2. George was often on those patrols since the patrols usually were able to get close enough to German outpost positions to hear conversations between soldiers. George would often creep dangerously close to try to pick up any scrap of information that could be overheard between unsuspecting German soldiers. George would sometimes lay still in the same spot for hours, paying no mind to the numbing cold, hard ground and sometimes steady drizzle. Most times he would wait until the German soldiers rotated shifts, hoping that a change in outpost personnel would lead to unchecked conversations or remarks that would bear fruit, although rarely did that happen. Eventually he would slowly work his way back to the others who were waiting to provide protective covering fire should he or they be spotted. They never were and would return to headquarters in Eschweiler with little to show for their efforts. Still, the patrols were able to verify that indeed from what they were able to hear, there seemed to be a continual flow of German traffic behind their lines. Their information, along with what was volunteered by the locals, was passed up the chain of command and sent on to headquarters where for reasons unknown it was set aside and deemed unreliable.

Call it distrust or cynicism, Captain Meisenhelter had a gut feeling that despite what G2 was saying, German troop and mechanized movements were attempts at shoring up defensive positions in anticipation of an allied advance into Germany, and that the German army was all but beaten and preparing for a "last stand", that this recent non-stop activity was something more. The feeling he had that made the hairs on the back of his neck tingle with an uneasy warmth from time to time, fueled by reports of frequent enemy reconnaissance patrols, leading him to believe that the Germans were building up and planning for some sort of an attack. Exactly what that attack would be, at what strength, where it would occur and when it might happen he didn't know and had no proof of, but until it could be proven otherwise or he knew what was going on, he ordered the entire HQ company to billet together for security reasons.

A week after St. Nicolas day George and Cletus left the parsonage across from St. Mauritius and returned to a second floor room in the Pletschet house. Spread between the Pletschet and Huberty houses, the entire HQ company was now together and would remain so until whatever that feeling was that the Captain had, passed. Two days later, on December 16th, reports began flooding into divisional headquarters that the Germans were attacking at various points along the front; the size of their forces and the scope of the attack was unclear. Word quickly spread that the 110th Regiment recently put under the command of WWI veteran Lt. Col. Hurley Fuller, was under attack in Clervaux, and although caught by surprise, the 110th was fighting back, keeping the Germans in check. Headquarters in Wiltz continued to receive reports from outposts and defensive positions that told of a massive enemy assault. German armored divisions and infantry was reportedly pouring through in spots along the entire 80 mile front being tenuously held by American troops. Now hating that feeling he had, Capt. Meisenhelter received orders that put the 28th Cavalry Reconnaissance Troop on full alert.

Top Left: George Mergenthaler; Bottom Left: Cletus LaFond; Top right: George, Charles Stansbury, Cletus LaFond; Bottom right: George, Charles & Cletus with an M-8, St. Mauritius in the background. Photos taken by Father Antoine Bodson, December 1944

Photos: LaFond Family Collection

TWELVE

Refugees began pouring into and through Eschweiler hoping to escape the death and destruction that was coming. Townspeople became anxious and began packing whatever they could, joining the refugees fleeing westward on the Wiltz-Bastogne road. Meantime with action reports flooding into the CP in Eschweiler, the Recon Troop was ordered to prepare for a defense of the town "at all costs". M-8 armored vehicles were deployed through the village, as were mortar and machine gun jeeps. However the Recon troop strength was initially compromised by divisional orders that sent 3rd platoon to man two divisional CPs near the front lines in the towns of Lieler, northeast of Clervaux, and Bastendorf, southeast of Wiltz, with the men of the platoon split between the two CPs. Their assignment was to help direct artillery fire where needed to stem whatever German push was occurring in that sector. The problem was that the cold front that had begun moving into the area brought the skies low, preventing any clear targeting of enemy positions. Later that same day 2nd platoon was tasked with establishing and holding a roadblock just a few miles northeast of divisional headquarters in Wiltz in the tiny crossroads town of Lellingen. Meantime the Recon soldiers remaining in

Eschweiler manned forward positions ringing the town while constant foot patrols probed the surrounding woods and roads for signs of any enemy activity. M-8s were also placed on the roads leading into town, their positions camouflaged for maximum effectiveness. Rumbles of artillery heard in the distance were drawing nearer.

The following day, on December 17th, 2nd platoon was ordered further east to secure a crossroad in the small town of Kautenbach, a few miles southeast of Wiltz, leaving only the headquarters platoon to defend Eschweiler. By the end of the day however, the soldiers of the 3rd platoon returned to town having narrowly escaped a formidable German onslaught that overran their positions at their respective divisional CPs. By this time Clervaux and the entire 25-mile stretch of front defended by Fuller's regiment was under heavy attack with the Germans making a hard push westward. The 28th Division headquarters was next in their sights. By the end of the day, all communication with the 110th regimental headquarters in Clervaux had been lost. There too the orders were to hold the town "at all costs". Earlier in the day Col. Fuller had ordered "anyone who can find a weapon" to take up defensive positions throughout the town. If forced to fall back, the soldiers would make their last stand at the castle.

Fighting with only two of the three brigades under his command, Fuller made a desperate phone call to divisional headquarters in Wiltz, asking for his remaining brigade that was being held in reserve. Fuller argued that the reserve troops needed to be sent to Clervaux immediately to help shore up his weakening defense of the town. Despite the irony of taking machine gun fire from a Tiger Tank that rolled past his headquarters in the Hotel Claravallis at the very moment he made the call, further emphasizing his desperation, his request was denied. Divisional command still clung to misguided belief that the assault on Clervaux could be a diversion and was hesitant to commit the few remaining reserve troops they had. Fuller and what now remained of his 110th were on their own. Now with all communications lost and needing to know the situation in Clervaux,

Captain Meisenhelter received orders from divisional HQ to send a patrol up to the town to find out what was happening and if possible to reestablish communications.

Riding in the lead jeep of two, Charles Jones and Joe Kost were among the seven men traveling north along narrow, muddied roads under pitch black skies when they approached a crossroads on the northern outskirts of Clervaux at around 11pm. Already zeroed in, the Germans immediately opened fire on the crossroad with anti-tank guns. The two jeep convoy was forced to quickly spin around on the tight roadway in the ink black night and attempt to retreat. Small arms fire now joined the anti-tank bursts. Turned around and starting back, the jeeps dodged repeated shell bursts when a shell exploded just a few feet in front of the second jeep, now in the lead. The concussive force of the blast knocked one of the soldiers riding in the back, out of the vehicle. From the passenger seat of his now trailing jeep Jones watched as the soldier tumbled down the steep roadside ravine and disappeared into the black pool of night. Stopping would have been suicide and the jeeps never let up, continuing their race back to Eschweiler. Well north of town the Recon jeeps passed through a roadblock guarded by Merg and Cletus with Stans in the turret of his M-8. Arriving back into Eschweiler just after midnight, the men immediately reported to headquarters that Clervaux had fallen into enemy hands. The news delivered, the exhausted soldiers found space on the floor of a now abandoned café on the outskirts of town to rest for a few hours. In the spacious Pletschet farmhouse, every bit of floor space was taken by sleeping, exhausted refugees.

Just after sunrise on the 18th of December, German infantry with armor support were attempting to push into Eschweiler from the southeast. Kost, Jones and the five other soldiers in the café were awakened by mechanized sound of approaching troops. Kost rallied quickly, grabbing a bazooka that had been in one of the jeeps. He darted out the back of the café, Jones following right behind with the few bazooka rockets he hastily grabbed. Ahead Kost eyed a small roadside retaining wall shouldering a bend in the road where he thought he could take cover while still having a full view of the road. German voices mixed with the groan of an engine and the tell tale squeak of tank treads. Kost and Jones knew they had one chance to stop, or at least delay the approaching Germans. Peering carefully over the wall Kost saw the frightening sight of a Panzer tank rounding a gradual turn in the road and coming into full view no more than 70 yards away. In order to make the approach to Eschweiler however, the tank would have to negotiate a hard 90-degree uphill turn only a few dozen yards up the road from where Kost and Jones were now crouched and waiting on the narrow, muddied road. Kost reasoned that as the Panzer slowed to negotiate the turn it would present their best and probably only chance at stalling the tank at worst and hopefully delaying the German attack. Kost and Jones were also relying heavily on the element of surprise that seemed to be in their favor. Staying low, and waiting probably longer than they dared to reveal their position, they could feel the ground beneath them shuddering and heard the engine roaring louder as the armored behemoth lumbered closer. The sharp turn in sight, the tank slowed in preparation for the turn, just as Kost had expected. He reared up and leveled the bazooka, the hulking mass of armor now nearly broadside and no more than twenty yards away. In the turret the commander saw the American soldier pop up but had no time to react or call out. The rocket zipped through the air, exploding into the side of the tank just below the turret, showering the road with flaming shrapnel. The only-stunned beast lurched, and then stalled, the commander no longer visible. Kost's well placed rocket hit the tank in one of the few vulnerable spots where bazooka rockets at close range could be effective against the otherwise formidable armored foe.

Other Recon soldiers who had taken cover and were waiting for their moment, now opened fire on the exposed trailing German infantry. Some fell immediately, their war ended, while the others dispersed in retreat. With machine-like precision Jones reloaded the bazooka. He tapped Kost's helmet. Kost aimed and squeezed the trigger. The second rocket hit its mark, one of the forward most wheels on the tank's port side, the roaring explosion blasting apart the tank's ribbon of tread. Again Jones moved quickly with an economy of motion; the bazooka again ready with a fresh round. Their third and last rocket exploded into the side of the Panzer. Burning and unable to move, the tank was now a 26-ton road block. German infantry scattered in retreat while Kost, Jones and the others scrambled up the road, then ran through patches of woods and finally across open pastures as they made their way back to Eschweiler more than a mile away.

With the fighting steadily drawing near, the people of Eschweiler began leaving en masse, hoping to stay ahead of the rapidly advancing Germans. Kost, Jones and the other soldiers made it to Eschweiler as some of the Recon vehicles prepared to pull out of town and as George and a handful of other soldiers and villagers exited St. Mauritius. A final mass was said with George and the others taking communion before getting to the business of war. The few remaining townspeople gathered outside the church in the cold morning air to say their goodbyes to the American soldiers who had become family in the month they'd been there. Tears flowed freely from soldiers and civilians alike; hugs and kisses exchanged. One last troop transport truck stood ready to evacuate those who held out as long as they dared, hoping it was all a bad dream, but now facing the harsh reality.

Frumpish once again, Virginia paused to say goodbye to George before jumping up onto the truck. She said nothing nor did he. No words would ever be enough. He looked at her and smiled as only George could; a smile that was at once reassuring and comforting, and also yearning and loving. Her eyes glistened, her lips tightened into thin strips. He tried to speak but before he could she threw her arms around his neck and held him tight, pressing her cheek into his neck, her tears leaving their mark on his collar. He wrapped an arm around her tiny waist, his other hand pressing firmly into the middle of her back, drawing her close, the smell of her hair intoxicating and a smell he'd never forget. Together they stood, their embrace locking out the world. At this moment there was no one else; there was nothing else. If only they could hold onto each other long enough, maybe this could all be over. Maybe just one embrace, *this* embrace could put an end to this madness that, yes had brought them together, but was now forcing them apart for God only knows how long? At this moment she knew she loved him. At this moment he knew no matter what he'd come back for her when the war ended. The throaty truck engine revved sending up a plume of black smoke. Slowly they parted, never taking their eyes off each other. Again George wanted to speak but she shook her head. She smiled at him then turned quickly and hopped up onto the truck.

Father Bodson was also in tears as he turned to say goodbye to George, the soldier that in just a few weeks he came to know as a brother. George put an arm around the priest.

"Don't worry Father, we'll drive them back," George comforted.

Father Bodson nodded. He knew George was right; they would drive the Germans back but when and at what price. The priest shivered with fear not knowing the answer to either question yet anticipating the worst. They shook hands and then he helped the priest climb up into the truck. The driver found first gear with a grind and the truck pulled away with George watching the two people he cared about most in the world at that moment disappearing down the road.

The sounds of the battle drew nearer. Dim splashes of orange light from the now not so distant artillery shells reflected off the low hanging grey clouds that loped in overnight, bringing with them cooler temperatures. The rumbles of thunder-like explosions rolled endlessly through the hills; shades of the Huertgen. The crackle of small arms fire could now be heard all around. North of town, the Germans were pushing through the woods and making their way along available roads but meeting stiff resistance from Recon Troop soldiers holding a line of defense. Although dramatically outnumbered, the Americans repeatedly beat back the Germans troops but the overwhelming number of enemy infantrymen advancing behind supporting armor meant they wouldn't be able to hold out much longer, and ammunition was running low. Gradually this company of Recon troop soldiers was forced to yield to superior numbers, but did so only after buying enough time for the rest of the troop to gather and retreat from Eschweiler.

Meantime all communication with divisional headquarters in Wiltz was lost when the town began taking direct enemy fire. Every effort was made to hold the line and stave off the enemy advance. Divisional headquarters soldiers usually tasked with only administrative duties, along with regimental cooks, MPs, replacement soldiers and even the 28th Infantry Division band were all pressed into the fight, trying to hold the line and stop the German advance. Despite their tenacity and courage, they were simply outmanned and outgunned. It quickly became clear that like Clervaux, where the main body of the 110th Regiment had been positioned, Wiltz and the 28th Division headquarters would soon fall to the Germans. A tactical withdrawal west towards Bastogne was ordered.

In Eschweiler, following orders given before communications were lost, the headquarters and 3rd platoons, all that remained in town, readied themselves to aid the 28th Infantry Division's headquarters unit's withdrawal from Wiltz a few miles to the south. George had been told by some of the refugees that the Germans had almost reached Café Halt, a crossroads that sat midway between Eschweiler and Wiltz and was named for the café that had stood overlooking the intersection for more than a century. At first it seemed incredible to the Recon troop that the Germans were able to advance that quickly until an artillery shell hit the feed loft of the Pletschet barn, setting it ablaze and erasing any doubt. George and Cletus stood in the doorway of the Pletschet farmhouse watching the flames, knowing there was nothing that could be done. Together they took one last look around the house that for the most part had been their home for most of the month. The fighting had come to this tiny town, and George took a mental picture of all he saw, the farmhouse, the barn now in flames and the church he had come to love, hoping they would survive the destruction that was sure to come. Then out of the corner of his eye George spied something out of place. There on a table in the outer room sat a bowl of chocolate pudding, left out to cool before the Pletschet family made the final and obviously hasty decision to flee. George threw Cletus a puckish grin and made his way to the table. He grabbed a nearby wooden spoon and dug in.

"Seems a shame to let it all spoil. It's not like they're going to come back anytime soon," George reasoned.

Cletus simply stood in the doorway and laughed softly while shaking his head. The pudding was almost gone when they heard Recon troop machine guns outside the farmhouse opening up again, firing at pockets of German reconnaissance soldiers that had suddenly appeared from the tree line having moved in from the east. George and Cletus joined the rest of the Recon Troop's headquarters company as well as soldiers from 3rd platoon readying to leave town in a convoy comprised of six vehicles: a radio jeep, a mortar jeep, the command jeep, a machine gun jeep, an M8 and a transport truck.

Capt. Meisenhelter and Lt. Hughes had a brief discussion on the best route out of town and best tactics to get them to Wiltz. Meisenhelter felt it would be best to avoid the route south as it was the more traveled route and would no doubt be the road the Germans would most likely use to push into Eschweiler. It was also near to where Kost and Jones had disabled the Panzer tank earlier in the day and it was still blocking the road the troop could become easy targets for the enemy.

Meisenhelter's idea was to take the road leading northeast away from town then swing back down towards Wiltz and to do so in two small groups, reasoning that if one group ran into trouble, the fight would allow the other a chance to push onto Wiltz. However Lt. Hughes countered that most of the German activity so far was concentrated in the fields and woods north and east of town, meaning that any attempt to move in that direction would mean they could be driving straight into the German advance. He also was convinced that moving in a compact convoy would give them better firepower should they run into trouble. The distinct high-pitched whistle from another salvo of incoming German mortars ended the discussion as the soldiers dove for cover.

Through the soft, wind blown snow, almost imperceivable as it fell, that now hung in the air mixing with the smoke from exploded shells and burning buildings, the Recon soldiers could just about make out the gray shapes of German troops moving through the thickly treed forest well beyond the fields south and west of town. The Recon soldiers again opened fire on the enemy soldiers, trying to pen them into the distant and dense woods. Jeep mounted machine-guns chattered out steady lethal streams, while the mortar jeeps pounded away at the trees and the M-8's fired their 37mm cannons at targets of opportunity in the treeline. The Germans, it now appeared, were coming in from all directions. Capt. Meisenhelter knew that if they didn't move immediately the entire Recon Troop risked being completely surrounded.

"We're getting outta here," he yelled, motioning to the road south, the same road Lt. Hughes had suggested and now looking like the quickest and possibly the only way out of Eschweiler. Most of the men of the headquarters and 3rd platoons, who had been firing from positions of cover in town towards any movement in the woods, secured their weapons and prepared to set out. Others, including Lt. Hughes, took their chances away from the convoy, running through the fields towards the cover of the woods west of town.

The remaining Recon Troop platoons, scattered at various points around the perimeter of town, valiantly tried as long as possible to beat back German soldiers, who were now attacking with superior numbers and armor support. With perimeter defenses collapsing, soon they too would be forced to withdrawal in any direction that seemed promising. As soon as they saw the line of incoming German tanks barreling towards them through the fields to the north, a company of men that had been holding a position on the road leading northeastward out of town, scrambled into their two jeeps and sped away from Eschweiler. This was the route Capt. Meisenhelter had suggested. SSgt. Chandler Capps, in command of the company, could see the rapidly approaching tanks leveling their guns, but the Recon soldiers, speeding and weaving around tight corners and horseshoe bends on the wet, muddy road made poor targets. The men would make it to Wiltz where, after reporting on the situation in Eschweiler, they were folded into a group of about a hundred soldiers pressed into defending the 28th Infantry Division's HQ company's withdrawal from town.

As Chandler and the others were speeding away from Eschweiler, at the other end of town the remaining Recon Troop soldiers were hastily forming their six vehicle convoy. Merg, as usual, hopped into the back of the command jeep, positioning himself behind the captain who sat in the passenger seat with Cpl. George Raduykavich was at the wheel. As the convoy formed, they ended up being the third jeep in the line of vehicles. Cletus climbed into the back of the mortar jeep being driven by Cpl. Carl Hess, the next in line behind the command jeep, while Stans assumed his position as the M-8 driver, and the rest of the four-man crew took up their positions. Their M-8 weaved into the convoy behind the mortar jeep Cletus was in. In the lead was another headquarters jeep that SSgt. Richard Sheesley managed to jump onto at the last moment as the convoy formed, and behind them, second in line, was the radio jeep driven by Joe Vocasek.

With the convoy moving as fast as they dared on the rain and snow slicked road, Merg tossed a last look back towards Eschweiler. Seeing the town that had been their home for the past month fade from view, through building mist he could see gray and some white coated soldiers appearing from the distant tree line, making their way across open fields towards the now deserted town. The light snow began to mix with freezing rain that rode in on stronger wind gusts. The convoy serpentined along the winding road while in the distance, the soldiers caught glimpses of enemy troops moving through the clusters of dense woods in what seemed like all directions. The Recon Troop soon realized that had they remained in Eschweiler much longer they would have been completely encircled.

After more than a mile the convoy finally approached a bend in the road after which stands of pines and hardwood trees framed the road giving them at least some cover until they rounded the ambling curve in the road as they approached Café Halt. From there a hard right turn would send them heading due south for a little more than two miles to Wiltz, or as close as they could get. The men scanned the woods framing the road on either side. Flashes of gray were all around. As the convoy began to clear the curve only a few hundred yards from Café Halt, German tanks from the 2nd Panzer Division driving towards Eschweiler from the south came into view. Their escape route was now blocked. The lead jeep swerved at the sight of the tanks, dumping Sheesley into a ditch on the left side of the road while the jeep careened right, slamming into the rocky berm. The rest of the convoy came to an abrupt stop, with vehicles swerving to avoid colliding with one another. A moment later, from the thick woods sloping away on their left, German soldiers opened up on the halted convoy. The recon troop had driven straight into the spearhead of the advancing German attack in that sector. Bullets pinged off the jeeps, tore into trees and sent up bursts of dirt and road. It all happened so fast that many of the recon solders, cascading out of their vehicles and diving for cover, forgot their weapons. For the moment at least they had escaped with their lives. All except Carl Hess. In the driver's seat in what was now the middle of the stalled convoy, Hess was completely exposed to the initial fusillade from the trees. Bullets tore into him. He tumbled out of the jeep and onto the road alive but badly wounded, his olive drab army jacket quickly blackening. Merg and the others hit the ground on the right side of the convoy, using their stranded vehicles as shields. They were unable to get to Hess who despite his grave wounds was trying to claw his way out of the line of fire.

Using the jeeps as cover, some soldiers managed to scramble over the rocky berm and crawl behind the smattering of trees on the upslope to the right of the convoy, but they could move no further. Beyond those thinly spaced trees was thirty yards of open field that would expose them to unrelenting enemy fire before they could reach the relative safety of dense woods. Meantime, German mortars opened up on the convoy, targeting the trapped vehicles. A German soldier peered over the top of the slope then tossed a "potato masher" grenade at the M-8. Seconds later the grenade exploded, blowing out the wheel on the left front side of the M-8, the soldiers inside shaken but uninjured, the armor floor holding. The scout car was now disabled, trapped in the middle of the convoy and as far as the crew inside was concerned, about to become an armored coffin. Stans and the others inside their crippled vehicle knew they had to get out. They managed to scurry out without getting shot because the thick, black smoke from the burning left front tire of the M-8 shielded them from the view of German guns. Staying low they ran to the cover of the trees just seconds before a mortar shell blew the M8 apart, leaving an unrecognizable flaming hulk in its place. A moment later another mortar round exploded on the hood of the trailing troop transport truck, reducing it to scraps of flaming metal and burning tires, and also closing off any chance of a motorized escape to the rear. With few weapons, nowhere to run and the road back now blocked, the Recon troop was completely pinned down.

Merg, crouching low and pressing himself against the side of the command jeep, looked down the roadside and saw the clutter of GIs flattened against the ground and berm, while others plastered themselves against trees staying low out of the direct line of fire. A few other soldiers, believing they had no choice, took their chances against German bullets and desperately tried to belly-crawl across the open field towards the woods. Merg could see the bleakness of their situation and knew it wouldn't be long before they'd be overrun by the German infantry pushing through the woods. The tanks at the end of the road were about to make the turn in their direction. Bullets continued hissing through the air. Capture or death were their only options. Something had to be done. Everything seemed to slow, the moment ensconced in a dream-like swirl, the sounds of battle condensed into a deafening din, and yet for Merg in that instant there was sudden clarity. He took a deep breath then swallowed hard. In a blur of movement, Merg vaulted into the back of the command jeep, grabbed the handle of the 50 caliber machine-gun, cycled the action and brought the muzzle to bear on the German infested woods. Keeping the trigger pulled he sprayed the trees with deadly fire, sweeping the gun from side to side, aiming at anything that moved. Now it was the Germans diving for cover, keeping them from at least advancing up the eastward facing slope and overwhelming the recon soldiers.

"Go!" Merg yelled over his shoulder to the rest of the troop. "Make a run for it," he roared while working the machine-gun, spent brass bullet casings raining into the bed of the jeep. The Recon soldiers saw their chance. Cletus and the other weaponless soldiers dashed through the open field, trying to make it to the woods. Bullets sizzled the air around them. Some soldiers with rifles saw their chance to enter the fray and began returning fire. Others chose to flee. Then Merg's machine gun jammed. Immediately the Germans seized their opportunity and opened fire again, while trying to once again move up the steep slope. Merg, standing monument tall in the back of the jeep while trying to rethread the ribbon of bullets into the breech, was an easy target. The air around him sizzled; bullets pinged off various parts of the jeep. Along the slope, staying just below the line of sight, a German soldier crawled, creeping ever closer to Merg's jeep. Within "can't miss" range he reared up and fired a burst from his "burp" gun. Poor footing and bad aim sent the volley of bullets amiss, hitting only air, the jeep or trees on the other side of the road. Unfazed or unaware of the burst that had miraculously missed its intended target, Merg continued working to clear the jam.

"Somebody shoot that son-of-a-bitch!" Capt. Meisenhelter yelled, pointing at the burp gun German. Vocasek was already leaning into a thick trunked tree and aiming his M1 Garand. He triggered four quick shots at the son-of-a-bitch. The German let out a scream and rolled down the slope in pain, one of the bullets ripping through his left hand. That bought just enough time for Merg to finish clearing the jam, thread the ribbon of ammo and again cycle the action. Once more he cut loose with the .50 cal.

"Get the hell out of here!" Merg shouted between machine gun bursts, waving away Vocasek and the few recon solders still hunkered down. Out of the corner of his eye Merg glimpsed Carl Hess lying in the road, blood soaked and no longer moving. A rush of anger seized him. Merg yelled again, only this time it was something in German over the barrel of his sweeping machine-gun.

Another chance, and the others made use of it, peeling off into the cover of the woods to the steady crackling of the machine gun. Moments later the gun jammed again. Once more in a flurry of speed Merg attempted to clear the breech. Seconds ticked away at a glacial pace. His wounded hand now wrapped in a crudely fixed and blood soaked bandage, the German soldier, having once again crawled up the slope, was now cradling his gun in the crook of his elbow. He raised up and squeezed off another bust, this time with deadly accuracy. Bullets ripped into George, one hitting his neck, punching out a spray of pink. Instantly his body went limp and he collapsed over the .50 cal machine gun momentarily, before tumbling out of the jeep.

For the remainder of that day and night, the GIs from the Recon Troop tried to make their way westward, despite worsening weather and battle chaos. Of the 160 men of the 28th Cavalry

Reconnaissance Troop that left Eschweiler during the early stages of the "Bulge", including the 28 soldiers in the ill-fated convoy that left town on the afternoon of December 18th, only 29 enlisted men and one officer managed to make it to Neufchateau. The rest of the men from the Recon Troop were captured, except for two who were killed.

Although gravely wounded, having lost a good deal of blood, George was taken prisoner along with most of the soldiers from the convoy. Now POWs, the soldiers were stripped of their personal items and anything else the Germans decided they wanted. The GIs were then forced to clear the road of their burned out or abandoned vehicles so that German armor and infantry could continue their rapid advance. Once the road was cleared, Recon Troop soldiers were then ordered to collect all their weapons and dump them onto a pile in front of Café Halt. German soldiers then doused the weapons with petrol and set them ablaze. The Americans were then marched a mile or so down the road towards Wiltz and held captive in a small barn until they could be transported to POW camps in the east.

Merg was carried by two Recon Troop soldiers to a spot just up the road from where their convoy was ambushed, past some of their still smoldering vehicles as the echoes of battle moved ever further away. The two soldiers sat with Merg in an area where a patch of earth had been dug out, leveling the ground for artillery that was never deployed. One of the soldiers was a medic attached to the Recon Troop. Despite the lack of any medical supplies, those being confiscated by the Germans, he did what he could, given the conditions, to keep George alive at best, comfortable at least.

Their clearing tasks completed, the captured Recon Troop soldiers were marched away as a German officer approached the two soldiers and their wounded comrade. He began speaking to them in English and although struggling with his wounds, George replied in German. The two soldiers engaged in a brief conversation in German, George laboring with every word. George may have said something in the course of their exchange that troubled or angered the German officer, or perhaps the German officer considered the seriously wounded, German speaking American a security risk should he overhear orders or battle plans. Perhaps it was nothing more than the sanctity of power, and the unwavering faith in the clarity of cause it yields, to know that the severely wounded soldier wouldn't survive the journey eastward, deep into Germany and beyond into Poland with the other POWs. The German divined that the soldier wouldn't survive a lengthy incarceration in a POW camp void of any proper medical facilities. With calloused indifference, the officer drew his pistol, racked the slide, pointed it at George's forehead and pulled the trigger. The two American soldiers who had been caring for George were frozen with shock and fear. They'd just witnessed the execution of a wounded prisoner of war and their friend. They believed they were next. They raised their arms slowly, the universal silent plea imploring the German not to shoot. Impassively, barely noticing them, the German holstered his pistol and in perfect English as he turned away, ordered the two soldiers to quickly bury the body.

THIRTEEN

News of the devastating surprise attack by the Germans in the Ardennes was slow in arriving on the home front. On December 17th 1944, the day after the attack began, the Chicago Tribune ran a front page story updating the war in Europe by mentioning German troop movements in the area of the Ardennes but offering little detail. However as the days and the battle wore on, reports from the front would begin to reflect the enormity and gravity of the offensive. Just two days before Christmas, on Saturday, December 23rd, 1944, a full week after the attack began, the front page of the New York Times was splashed with this headline:

"GERMANS SWEEP WEST THROUGH LUXEMBOURG;
REPORT PATTON ATTACKING SOUTH FLANK;
EISENHOWER URGES GREATEST ALLIED EFFORT"

In Rye, NY, Herman and Alice Mergenthaler, like so many other parents, anxiously awaited word from their son. The last letter they received from George arrived just the day before but was dated December 3rd. It touched on benign topics: George talking about some of the people he met in the town they were in (not able to divulge his exact location per army regulations) and how welcoming the townspeople were; how he'd become "chummy" with the priest from the local church, then briefly describing St. Mauritius; how bad army chow was but that the priest's cook was quite good at turning army food mixed with whatever she could scrounge into something remarkably palatable; how he and the other soldiers took to working on the nearby farms to pass the time and how he finally learned how to milk cows, something not as easy as one would think. He once again thanked his parents for sending baked goods and that he now shared them with the people in the village especially the children who really had nothing; and he thanked his parents for expediting the items requested for the only days away celebration of St. Nicolas Day, the parcels arriving just that morning. He mentioned Christmas and how, although it didn't seem likely that the war would be over by then as was once the prevailing rumor, war's end seemed very possible by the new year according to the latest chatter.

Now, with the reveal of the German offensive, none of that or anything else mattered. They knew George was somewhere in Luxembourg but didn't know precisely where, making newspaper headlines and radio bulletins all the more jarring. Still they hoped that wherever he was it was out of harm's way. He, along with the rest of the division, was on R&R well west of the front lines, that much they knew. From what they'd read in the papers and heard on the radio they believed he'd be well away from the spearhead of the attack. However the lack of any new letters from George was alarming. Then again this was war, and this massive German offensive had no doubt disrupted any sort of normal military operations including mail delivery. Not content to simply sit and anxiously wait, Herman used whatever means at his disposal to gather any scrap of information on where his son might be. Political and business contacts were utilized to their fullest. Social connections were pressed; calls to various newspaper owners were made; favors called in, money spent. Despite his best efforts through numerous channels of influence, there simply was no news to be had. Even as the weeks mounted and the tide of war began to shift with the Americans having blunted the German advance sometime around Christmas, little was known about the fate of their only son, lending to speculation that he might have been captured and was now a POW. That, they reasoned, and prayed, would explain the lack of communication from George or any official notification on his whereabouts.

Postcards began arriving to anxious families in the States in mid-January. By that time captured soldiers from various outfits, including those of the Recon Troop, were now prisoners of war and had been marched east to several different POW camps. Upon arrival the POWs were registered with the International Red Cross, given metal, numbered ID tags and were allowed to send one postcard to their families. Charles Jones' card was dated January 9th but wouldn't arrive to his Tennessee home until more than two weeks later.

For the Mergenthalers, official notification finally came on Monday January 22nd, when a Western Union telegram from the War Department arrived further fueling their POW hopes. The one sentence telegram stated for the record that George Mergenthaler was "Missing in Action". Quick to pick up on the famous name, newspapers throughout the country ran various versions of the same story, none telling it better than the January 27th edition of the *New York Tribune*, the bold-faced headline perched atop the article reading:

"MERGENTHALER'S GRANDSON, 24, IS MISSING AT FRONT
Kin of Linotype Inventor Is Reported a Casualty in Action in Luxembourg"

The article, accompanied by George's Princeton University yearbook picture, offered no further details on his whereabouts. It did however mention a postcard the Mergenthalers received on January

25th, three days after the official War Department telegram arrived. The postcard too was dated December 3rd, and was from Belgian architect Mario Van Montfort. It read in part:

> *"I had the great pleasure to meet your son in action 'somewhere in Europe'. He was the first to arrive in a village where I was hiding waiting for the Jerries to go! Would you please send him our best wishes for Christmas and New Year's?*
>
> *He gave me his home address, but now, according to new regulations, we should be able to write to him and I would be delighted to have his army address. Tell him to write to us please, and to come to our home as soon as he can get leave.*
>
> *He talked a lot about yourself and we hope to hear of you very soon and have good news from both of you. And thanks a lot to the US Army."*

January 27th, 1945 was also the day that the face of Nazi Germany would be given a name that would forever symbolize absolute evil and hatred plumbed from the furthest depths of inhumanity: Auschwitz. The Russian army had been hammering German troops in the east, pushing the tattered remnants of the once mighty Wehrmacht back into Germany. As the relentless Russian advance neared the camp, SS troops, following orders to liquidate the remaining prisoners in an effort to conceal the true nature of the death camps, killed thousands before forcing more than 60,000 others on death marches westward. SS guards shot prisoners that fell behind or simply couldn't continue, while many others died from starvation or exposure. In all more than 15,000 prisoner died during the death marches from Auschwitz. On January 27th, the Russian army finally entered Auschwitz liberating the more than 7,000 prisoners that remained.

By this time the western front had returned to where they had been prior to the Battle of the Bulge, with the German army forced to retreat back into their homeland. Hitler's big gamble had succeeded only in delaying the inevitable invasion of Germany by a half-dozen weeks while sacrificing the bulk of his remaining army. The shredded 28th Infantry Division, having taken on the full throated assault from the beginning, continued to fall back to the southwest, finally digging their heels in at the town of Neufchateau in Belgium about 20 miles southwest of Bastogne. There remnants of various units gathered, regrouped and helped stop the German advance that had begun to wither due in part to over extended supply lines, the lack of fuel, depleted fighting forces, the superiority of Allied air support and tenacious fighting from weary but determined front line American soldiers.

Cletus, Stans, Gene McHale, Dan Garbo and Lt. Hughes were among the Recon Troop soldiers that managed to work their way through the snowy woods and roads, eventually meeting up with other stragglers and together pushing westward. Often they encountered German troops but chose to avoid them since few of the soldiers had weapons. However when stumbling upon German roadblocks that couldn't be bypassed, the group, relying on the element of surprise, would rush the soldiers on guard, overpower them and seize their weapons before continuing their trek to join the rest of the division. It was because of these heroic actions that Cletus and McHale were eventually awarded Bronze Stars, while Charles Stansbury would be awarded a Silver Star.

At the beginning of February refugees forced to flee their homes and lands ahead of the German attack were now beginning to return. The people of Eschweiler, most of whom had fled south and well west of the battle, journeyed through towns and cities, now reduced to piles of rubble save for a few skeletal building facades, burnt but standing stubbornly as if refusing to fall in protest to the bitter war. Roads were littered with the snow-covered remnants of once mighty war machines creating a macabre landscape, a sobering reminder of the vicious fighting and the blood spilled in the fight for freedom. On February 5th, a group of townspeople approached Eschweiler and after all they'd seen, feared the worst.

The Pletschet barn was razed as were several homes, victims of direct artillery strikes leaving snow covered piles of rubble and bits of blackened wood beams and furniture in their stead, the smell of old smoke and decay carried on the valley's winter wind. The other buildings in town were all scarred by bullets and shrapnel, with those closest to the main roads most heavily damaged but, at least, still standing. Overall there was surprise and some relief as the townspeople were able to return to their homes. Except for the few cows, pigs and chickens they fled and returned with, the rest of Eschweiler was devoid of any livestock, most of it pillaged by the retreating Germans though some remained, now soft undulations in the otherwise flat snowy pastures.

People from Eschweiler pose for a picture with the Sherman tank; St. Mauritius in the background, July 1945

Photo: National Archives

Father Bodson walked past the snow covered M4A4 Sherman tank, one of three that had been dispatched to try to hold Eschweiler during the early fighting of the "Bulge". This one had broken down during the fighting and the crew, unable to make repairs while coming under direct enemy fire, continued their defense as an armored pillbox, firing the 75mm cannon and machine guns at German troops trying to push into town from the woods and road from the south. German tanks and infantry would eventually overwhelm those desperately trying to defend the town, and this five-man tank crew was forced to flee, abandoning their Sherman where it remained still, on the side of the road just steps from St. Mauritius.

The priest first noticed the bullet marked west facing wall, the damage pattern drawing his eyes to the window openings that once held richly colored stained glass. Now only the most stubborn shards clung to the edges of their leaded frames, the empty windows vacant, soulless. Looking up at the spire, more damage from bullet and shrapnel: holes punched through, roofing shingles broken or missing. "Let that be the most of it", the priest prayed, hoping that the church, like most of the buildings in town, had only suffered minor, easily repairable damage. Walking around to the front of the church, one of the double doors to the vestibule showed bullet and shrapnel damage, the other was missing completely. Entering into the vestibule the priest's heart fell. Broken pew benches, toppled marble and wood statues and pedestals, and broken glass were all covered by a thin layer of snow that winter winds had whipped around the interior of the church. From the holes in the roof and spire, water damage and the freeze/thaw cycle over the past six weeks had taken a toll on everything, but especially the brightly colored mural behind what remained of the smashed altar, where rivulets of water had peeled away the paint and plaster in streaks. Across from the altar, just inside the front doors, crushed and broken organ pipes were strewn about. Some pipes were missing, no doubt plundered by German soldiers looking to loot anything of value or use. Still, the church was able to provide some shelter and at some point, with no other suitable buildings left standing to house the few remaining farm horses that had survived the fighting, the church was used to stable them from the harsh winter. Judging by conditions, the horses had been kept there for quite some time. Above those horses, in the loft, the church organ was heavily damaged; the keys smashed, more pipes broken or crushed, and the wood on one side of the instrument studded with shrapnel. In the parsonage across the road, while some books were still on shelves, most were scattered throughout the great room. Some it appeared were burned in the stove for warmth. The furniture had been rearranged but most of it was unbroken. All the windows however were smashed, apparently to allow soldiers to shoot through. Here too whatever was deemed valuable in any way was looted. Of all the buildings in Eschweiler still standing, the one most severely damaged during the fighting was St. Mauritius.

While the people of Eschweiler were returning home, what was left of the 28th Cavalry Recon Troop, still officially assigned to the 28th Infantry Division, was ordered to areas around the town of Colmar in the Alsace region of France, bordering Germany. Here the Germans were putting up a desperate defense as the Allies made their way eastward toward the Rhine River. The Recon Troop, steadily being refortified with equipment and replacement personnel, at various times during the month acted as liaisons between the 12th Armor Division and the 110th Regiment by maintaining communications as both units pushed onto the Rhine just south of Colmar. The Recon troop also served as additional protection for the regiment's right flank and established contact with French Rangers, aiding them with the defense of the town of Wintzenheim just west of Colmar. They established roadblocks and roving patrols throughout the area that was still seeing pockets of dwindling but fierce German resistance. By the end of February Allied forces had beaten the Germans back across the Rhine and were driving onto Berlin.

Meantime in Rye, NY daily calls to the post office proved

fruitless for Herman and Alice Mergenthaler who were desperate for any news of their only son. There were no letters from George or any communications from the army. Massaged business, political and social contacts yielded nothing. It had been more than a month since he'd been reported missing and more than two since they received his last letter. As February eked by, although vowing to remain optimistic without any word whatsoever, their hope slowly ebbed and they steeled themselves for the worst while praying for the best.

It wasn't until the middle of March that the snows from the worst winter the Ardennes had seen in decades finally began melting on a wave of steadily warming weather. By then the people of Eschweiler had begun what would be a slow process to rebuild their lives and their community. At St. Mauritius, everyone helped when they could with whatever they could. The most immediate repairs needed were to keep the elements at bay to prevent further damage. Army supplied tarps were used to cover the holes in the roof; cloth scavenged from disabled and abandoned army trucks and tenting material was nailed over the windows; the interior of the church was cleared of debris; statues not too badly broken were repaired. The altar would be replaced by boards placed over saw horses. There was no telling when new stained glass windows could be made, the wall and roof fixed properly, a new altar built and the organ repaired. For mass, people brought chairs from their homes while Father Bodson worked to repair those that could be fixed. There was no heat and no light. Candles and oil lamps would have to do. For now, and for who knows how long, this would be St. Mauritius.

While parishioners in Eschweiler tended to their church, the Recon Troop was on the move for most of March. From the Colmar region in France they worked their way northeastward, at times traveling over the same ground and roads veteran members of the troop had crossed during the Bulge. Still charged with establishing and maintaining rear guard defensive positions, conducting road patrols and occasionally manning forward observation posts in relief of front line soldiers, the troop moved through towns in France and Belgium before arriving into the German town of Niedermendig, fourteen miles due west of Koblenz on the 19th of March. There they would remain until the end of the month, once again providing rear guard support for the division.

The spring sun was shining bright and warm on the afternoon of Saturday March 24th, 1945 slowly pulling a stubborn blanket of snow down into the earth and muddying the road that Suzanne Arens, whose family owned Café Halt, and five year old Raimond Streicher now walked on their way from the café to Eschweiler. After such brutal winter cold with the sun's rays washing over her face, Suzanne allowed her mind to wander, thinking how the annual flowers she had planted in their garden years ago would once again fight their way through the cool soil; It wouldn't be long now before the snows would finally give way to the grassy fields anxious to awaken from winter's slumber. Just a few weeks from now, the buds that seemed so easy to see on the tips of tree branches, would burst forth and overnight transform the hills into a rolling sea of green.

What brought her mind back from its wander were the small, neatly shaped patches of white along the roadside that Raimond had found. At first they appeared to be perfectly formed rectangles of snow that for some odd reason hadn't melted. Moving closer she realized that what the curious, little boy had picked up were soggy photographs, their white backs reflecting the afternoon sun. As she shuffled through the pictures a jolt of panic and fear, then a rush of burning took her breath away. She knew these pictures, she'd seen them before, they all had: the woman in the wedding dress, the older couple in the garden, the color picture of the handsome soldier standing in front of Christmas roses. In shock, she searched for a reason these pictures were here. Perhaps he'd been captured, and maybe the German soldier who had searched him tossed them away. Maybe he had discarded them during the fighting for some reason or maybe they just fell out of his pocket. Maybe he left them here, maybe under a rock or something to retrieve later. Maybe he tossed them here as a message to everyone in Eschweiler that he was ok, that he'd be back. At that moment each explanation seemed plausible to her and she desperately wanted to believe any one of them. Maybe. Her eyes darted around the road. Perhaps there was something else nearby that could explain more. A wallet? Letters? Papers? More pictures? She told Raimond they were playing a game and to keep looking. "Find something and there will be a prize." The boy eagerly searched for more.

The way the sunlight shone through the pines at just that moment, to that now snowless area to the right of the elbow bend in the road, couldn't have been by chance. It glinted off the edge of the helmet carefully placed on the elongated pile of rocks that had been covered by winter until now. Though she'd seen more death in these last five years than a young woman should ever see, the site of this crudely but carefully fashioned grave made her shudder. She paused staring at the stones, then at the photos. She and the boy trotted the remaining mile up the winding, muddy road to the Huberty house. Shivering and gasping for breath she told Virginia what she'd found. She showed her the pictures. Virginia's eyes welled as she examined the photographs longer than needed, playing for time, praying for a miracle. She looked up and bit her lip, hard. She sighed deeply then bounded out the door and trotted down the same muddy road towards the church.

She was almost at the church steps when Father Bodson stepped out from the vestibule. At first he cast her a smile but her ashen face, expressionless, made him uneasy. He cocked his head and was about to ask if she was alright when he saw her eyes begin to glisten. He noticed the pictures she still held and his face fell. He slowly rolled his head from side to side in disbelief. He was suddenly aware of his own breathing. His throat tightened and he swallowed hard.

"Where?" he breathed, resigned.

Virginia explained, then accompanied the priest down the road. They walked slowly in silence. There was nothing that could be said. Twenty minutes later they reached the bend in the road and they saw the spot Suzanne had mentioned and the helmet resting atop the rocks. For a few moments they stood unable to move. The priest's hands, balled into fists, were stuffed into his pockets. He took a deep breath then let it out slowly. She felt a crushing sensation in her chest as she fought back the tears, waiting on the side of the road while he slowly approached the makeshift grave. Kneeling down, he whispered a short prayer then moved the helmet aside. Of course he knew, but he needed to be certain. Virginia watched as the priest began pulling away the rocks one by one until he exposed the head of the body beneath. Time, wound and winter had taken their toll leaving the face unrecognizable. A few more stones were removed exposing a mat of hair. He recognized it immediately. His shoulders slumped; she sobbed uncontrollably. He muttered a quick prayer then searched around the neck for ID tags but there were none. He removed more stones exposing the soldier's left arm. The priest felt around the cold, gray wrist, looking for the silver ID bracelet he wore all the time, the one Herman had given him at the train station before shipping out, the one engraved with his name, hometown and army serial number. There was no bracelet. A spoil of war, it had been taken months ago by the Wehrmacht soldier from Austria who, with his blood-soaked bandaged hand, stood guard while the two American soldiers did as ordered and buried the body.

More stones were removed. The priest unzipped the soldier's soggy jacket hoping to find ID tags in a shirt pocket. He shuddered and a moment later wept at the sight of the purple sweater. He fought the tears and the feeling of utter emptiness by whispering another prayer, imploring the Lord to accept his dear friend into heaven. The priest patted the body searching for any personal items and found only the metal army ID tags that someone had stuffed into a shirt pocket beneath the sweater, in the same pocket that held George's prayer book. In another pocket he found George's reading glasses. Thinking it through, the young priest gathered himself while gathering the stones that had been removed. He placed them back over George's body. Carrying the helmet, he and Virginia walked back up the road to Eschweiler.

They were almost at the church when they saw people beginning to gather in front of the steps leading to the vestibule. Word had already spread throughout the small town about the grave and about the photos. With words he at first struggled to find then struggled to speak, Father Bodson confirmed to those gathered what they had feared. As far as anyone in Eschweiler was concerned, one of their own, a victim of this horrible war, was just discovered buried beside the road leading to town. Everyone stood for a few moments, perhaps praying silently. Finally the priest cleared his throat. There would be more time to grieve, he announced, but right now there was work to do and with that he disappeared into St. Mauritius while Virginia made the long walk to her home just up the road.

Father Bodson took charge, hastily but carefully planning the events to come, doling out tasks to everyone wanting to be involved and ensuring that all details were covered. Two of those details involved traveling to nearby Wiltz the following day, where he alerted the army of the discovery of George' body, and waited until he received permission from Army administrators to bury George in the church cemetery, assuring the unimpassioned soldier routinely jotting down the information that the town of Eschweiler would see to a proper burial. His last task before leaving Wiltz was the purchase of a simple pine coffin.

Cletus LaFond was busily compiling and typing after action reports that had piled on his clerk's desk when the phone rang. Lt. Hughes, on the other end of the line, cleared his throat then got to the reason for the call.

"Listen, they found a body back in Luxembourg, in that town...Eschweiler," the Lieutenant stated factually, his words slicing into Lafond. "They want us to confirm the ID. What was Merg wearing when you last saw him?"

The hair on the back of Cletus' neck tingled, a mix of warmth and cool shot up his spine. He felt his eyes welling. He hesitated, knowing what the Lieutenant wanted to hear, as if not saying it wouldn't make it true. At once the memories of his friend darted through his mind. He and George in Wales, traveling through France, in Paris...Paris. Belgium, Germany and Luxembourg. Everything they'd seen together, everything they did together. Eschweiler; Thanksgiving at the parsonage, St. Nicolas Day, the church, the fields, *that* morning, the pudding...God George loved chocolate and sweets, the convoy. Again the Lieutenant cleared his throat.

"Do you recall what he had on", Hughes said trying to coax an answer from LaFond who he knew was struggling.

Cletus breathed deep, "Under his ODs...the purple sweater vest his mother made for him," he sighed in resignation.

"Yep, that's him alright," the Lieutenant replied, then after a short pause added, "Word is they found him buried in a shallow grave just outside of town. Didn't see the grave until the snows melted."

With that Cletus hung up the phone and pushed aside the reports. They could wait. He thumbed through the company casualty reports, pulling out the one with George's name on it. He stared at the paper, wishing it was another name, any other name than the one stamped onto the paper in black ink. A few minutes passed before Cletus finally made the change to the official army document, crossing out MIA and in the margin writing KIA.

Late in the afternoon on March 26th Father Bodson and other men from Eschweiler returned to the stone covered grave and exhumed the body of their friend. The priest removed the ID tags from the shirt pocket and using a piece of wire, secured one of the tags around George's neck while keeping the other tag to send home to George's parents. He then wrapped a set of rosary beads around George's hands before the body was wrapped in a sheet and placed into the coffin. He and the others said a prayer over George before the lid of the coffin was nailed shut. Men from Eschweiler, including Albert Nathieu, Albert Arend, René Danit and Pierre Pletschet, lifted the casket and carefully walked it to the road where the entire population of Eschweiler, save for the elderly and the sick, had gathered. Together the entire town, lead by altar boys Nicolas Zeien and Antoine Lanners and an honor guard comprised of the local boy scouts and their scout master, silently walked in a funeral cortege up the muddy road to the cemetery a mile away. Damage to the church would make a funeral mass impossible, instead a graveside service would have to suffice. At the gravesite, overlooking one of the fields where George had spent much of his time while in town, townspeople gathered to honor and pray for this fallen soldier, their friend. As the peeling bells of St. Mauritius sounded, the town prayed while George's coffin was lowered into a grave edged with a flower border and marked by a three foot tall, thick cement cross with George's name carved into its base. The cross was mounted onto a large two-tiered brick base, the mortar still not dry.

The funeral procession through Eschweiler, March 26th, 1945, led by altar boys Nicolas Zeien and Antoine Lanners

Photo: Nicolas Lucas, Eschweiler

(L-R) Albert Nathieu, Albert Arend, René Danit and Pierre Pletschet carrying George's coffin to the gravesite, March 26th, 1945

Photo: Nicolas Lucas, Eschweiler

The people of Eschweiler gathered around George's grave, March 26th, 1945

(Father Bodson is seen on the left edge of the picture)

Photo: Nicolas Lucas, Eschweiler

Photo: Nicolas Lucas, Eschweiler

FOURTEEN

Teresa Ball was the postmaster in the Rye, NY Post Office. Her son Cornelius was serving in the army as an MP, assigned as a driver for staff cars. During his time he drove for Generals Eisenhower, Bradley, Patton and Clark, often at night during blackouts. He too was caught up in the initial confusion of the Bulge. She, like everyone in Rye, knew that George was still missing and was the reason the Mergenthalers came into the post office every day to check their mail, hoping for a letter or postcard from George.

"Have you heard from your son?" Alice always asked graciously.

"Yes, thank you. he's ok. Still driving the generals around. Any word from George?"

"No, but I'm sure we will hear something soon," answered Alice, trying to sound convincing.

On the morning of March 30th, Teresa's daughter Audrey, working alongside her mother at the post office as a clerk, was sorting the day's incoming batch of mail when she spotted the official army letter addressed to the Mergenthalers. Teresa picked up the phone immediately and placed the call. Through a steady, cold spring rain shower Herman and Alice arrived at the post office a short time later. Teresa and her daughter watched the Mergenthalers open and read the letter that, despite prayers to the contrary, they knew was destined to come. Herman read it twice, the second time through pooling eyes. Wiping away her tears Alice thanked the postmaster and her daughter for the phone call. The Mergenthalers said nothing else as they left the post office arm and arm beneath the shelter of their umbrella.

The letter, while not wholly unexpected, left the Mergenthalers devastated. The unknown had given them hope; the letter had vanquished that hope, leaving an irreplaceable void. To conciliate their grief they wanted to find out as much as they could about how George had lived the last few weeks of his life, and just as importantly how he died. By pressing sympathetic political connections, Herman was able to get a brief report from the army, compiled from after action reports written by Lt. Hughes and typed by Cletus LaFond, that shed some light onto what happened that day. They discovered that George had been part of a Recon Troop company that had been ambushed during the Ardennes offensive and that he had been killed near Café Halt, just outside a town called Eschweiler in Luxembourg. Little else was known at the time since those who had witnessed George's heroic stand and ultimately his death were still being held as POWs. As for how he lived, they needed to turn to the person George mentioned frequently in his last few letters home: his close friend Father Bodson. Once more Herman used his influence with government officials to try to get in touch with the priest.

A week after George's burial Father Bodson received word from the Luxembourg government, from the office of the Prime Minister, that George's parents had been trying to find him. On April 10th Father Bodson wrote the first of what would be many letters to the Mergenthalers, each offering glimpses into the final weeks of their son's life. In his first letter Father Bodson told them of how George spent many days and nights in the parsonage, sharing meals, listening to the radio, talking for hours about his home, and how George always assisted with morning mass and took communion. He mentioned how they'd spent Thanksgiving together and how George always insisted on opening packages from home in front of him, then sharing whatever was sent with everyone in town. He told them how George came to think of the parsonage and the town as a whole as his home. He told them how everyone knew George by the wonderful purple sweater she had knitted him. He also told them about the last time he saw George, how they shook hands, wept, then parted on the morning of December 18th. He further explained how sad he was when he found George's body in the roadside grave, knew it was him from the sweater. He told them how he had purchased a coffin and how all the parishioners were there when they reburied George in the church cemetery as they would one of their own. The letter went on to reassure the grieving parents as best he could that George was a good son, well liked by all he met and that he'd received communion the very morning he died, and that he was surely in heaven, where they would all meet again someday.

That letter began a steady correspondence between Father Bodson and the Mergenthalers, who over time came to accept the priest as part of their family, as another son. In subsequent letters the priest detailed the funeral of their son and described where he was now buried. He also sent the Mergenthalers the photos he took of George just days before he died, his ID tag and his prayer book and photos taken at the time of the funeral. Despite the town's outpouring of love for their son, and the insistence of Father Bodson that George's resting place was one of beauty and peace with a spectacular view of the valley George had come to love, Alice would never get over her loss and was determined to have George brought home to the Sweeney Family Plot at Holy Sepulchre Cemetery in Rochester, NY.

Through constant correspondence with the priest, the Mergenthalers came to understand how much their only son meant to the town of Eschweiler and the lasting friendships he'd made. They promised to visit Eschweiler one day, and although they fully intended to bring their son home and had in fact set in motion the necessary paperwork to accomplish the task, they more than anyone, understood what his loss meant. Therefore they were determined to do something for the town that had shown so much love for George during his final days, something that would leave them with a lasting memory of George. The idea was something they felt George would have insisted on had he lived: the Mergenthalers would fund the rebuilding of St. Mauritius.

A few weeks after the war in Europe ended in May of 1945, Herman contacted and commissioned a Belgian architect familiar with building and church designs of the area, someone he felt would embrace the project since he had in fact also known George: Mario Van Montfort. Local craftsmen, trade workers and artists were then hired to make repairs on the church, returning it to how it had been before the Bulge, using Van Montfort's design plans. Overseeing the entire project with its unique elements would fall to Father Bodson. Although the materials needed for the restoration were in short supply, Van Montfort used his connections with builders and material suppliers as well as black marketeers near and far to secure what was needed. Money was not a factor; creating a lasting memory of George was. Still it would take nearly two years for the project, often hampered by weather and supply delays, to be completed. By early 1947 St. Mauritius had been completely refurbished and updated, including the addition of a new heating system, new wiring and special lighting. The front doors that had been so severely damaged were replaced, as was all the church wiring, necessary to accommodate new lighting and a new heating system. Upon entering the vestibule, on the left wall visitors are met by a large round plaster disk with a life-sized cast of George Mergenthaler's face. Beneath the disk sits a bronze plaque, engraved in both English and French, that reads:

IN MEMORY OF
GEORGE OTTMAR MERGENTHALER
AUGUST 5, 1920 – DECEMBER 18, 1944
AMERICAN SOLDIER

GRANDSON OF OTTMAR MERGENTHALER
INVENTOR OF THE LINOTYPE

WHO FELL IN ACTION AT
ESCHWEILER LUXEMBOURG
DECEMBER 18, 1944

MAY THE RESTORATION OF THIS CHAPEL
BE OF SOLACE TO ALL
AS IT GAVE COMFORT TO OUR SON

ALICE AND HERMAN MERGENTHALER
RYE, NEW YORK

On the stark white wall above the plaster disk, black embossed letters in both English and Luxembourgish read:

"THIS ONLY SON DIED THAT OTHER SONS MIGHT LIVE IN LOVE AND PEACE"

Walking into the church one passes under the choir, supported by marble pillars, where the newly repaired organ with its the symmetrically arranged array of pipes stretches across the front wall while majestically thrusting skyward. Also at the front, the small chapels on either side of the transept, once severely damaged during the war, were repaired and updated as was the sacristy, matching the newly constructed and fortified interior walls sporting alternating gray and dark and light brown sandstone buttresses arching overhead. The stained glass windows had all been replaced, their luxuriant colors once again bathing the church in warm, comforting light. This time however the artwork of the window designs was changed from what they had been before the war. Now in one window, above a pattern of gold and white glass, sits the seal of Luxembourg, while another window with the same pattern holds the seal of the United States at the top, while at the bottom is the Mergenthaler family crest. Two other windows are specifically dedicated to the Mergenthalers, one dedicated to Herman and the other to Alice. In another window is an artist's depiction of St. Mauritius, while another window shows a bronze age soldier slaying a serpent with a spear, a ribbon of text above the soldier reading: S. GEORGIUS.

Below the windows, custom made oak bench pews sit atop charcoal gray slate tiles covering the floor of the nave and the sanctuary, where a heavy oak altar sits, the lamb of God carved into the front. Behind the altar towers a reredos of ornately carved grayish-brown marble where in a center niche a hand carved wooden statue of

St. Mauritius stands, a lance in his right hand, looking out over the congregation. Beneath the statue is the tabernacle, flanked by marble angels, a small statue of Christ on the cross between them. Above the altar, the high arched ceiling between the buttresses has been ornately hand painted with depictions of saints looking down from the heavens. Behind the altar, on either side of the marble altarpiece, the murals have been

repainted just as they had been prior the war. The left mural is a scene depicting Jesus preaching to the masses and healing the sick, while the one on the right depicts the miracle of loaves and fishes, with Christ feeding the masses aided by of one of his apostles; an apostle who, beneath his robe of brown and purple is wearing a green, American army jacket and bearing the likeness of George Mergenthaler.

ICH·BIN·DAS·LEBENDIGE·BROT·DAS·VOM·HIMMEL·GEKOMMEN
WER·VON·DIESEM·BROTE·ISST·WIRD·LEBEN·IN·EWIGKEIT

Of note:

When the war in Europe ended, Cletus LaFond returned to Paris to find Anne. The two were married in Paris in July,1945 and then moved to the States, eventually settling in Michigan.

Cletus, who was awarded a Bronze star for his actions during the Battle of the Bulge, died in 2004 at the age of 89.

In 1947, despite the town's wishes to the contrary, Herman and Alice Mergenthaler finally brought George home, where he was reburied in Holy Sepulchre Cemetery in Rochester, NY. It wasn't until years later, in 1954, that the Mergenthaler's finally made a point to visit the town that had embraced their only son. Alice never got over the death of George. Friends say she died of a broken heart on May 20th, 1962.

Eschweiler, 1954: photo taken by Alice Mergenthaler
Photo: Mergenthaler Family Collection

Herman lived in Rye, NY, for the rest of his life. Often he would visit Nora Mitchell (the girl he pulled from the Blind Brook) just to see how she was doing. He died in his home on the grounds of the Westchester Country Club on June 12th 1972.

Dan Garbo returned to Wales after the war to find Emma Friar waiting for him. The two were married in St. Mary's Church in St. Clears, and shortly after they moved to Dan's Chicago area home to start a family. A year later Emma died giving birth to the couple's daughter. Dan Garbo died in 1982 at the age of 63.

Virginia Huberty remained in Eschweiler until the 1960s, when she met and married a widower and moved to Brussels, Belgium. She frequently returned to Eschweiler to be with her family, especially on holidays. She died in Wiltz on October 28th, 1995 at the age of 83.

Nora Mitchell served during World War II at the British Embassy, handling confidential documents and overseas cables, including coded messages between Britain's Prime Minister Winston Churchill and President Roosevelt. On D-Day, June 6, 1944, she was assigned as an aide to the director of British Information Services and until 1946 was a member of the British delegation to international conferences that would eventually lead to the establishment of the United Nations. She married James E. Mitchell, an attorney with the US Department of Housing and Home Finance in 1949 and in 1955 they returned to Rye with their three daughters. She took a position as the assistant to the City Managers of Rye until she retired in 1986. Nora died on October 17, 2013 at the age of 95.

In May of 1949, at their urging, Father Antoine Bodson visited the Mergenthalers in New York, with whom he maintained a close relationship. During his time in the US he visited several communities of Luxembourgers around the country before returning to Eschweiler in July of that year. Two years later in 1951 he was transferred to a parish in Luxembourg Stadtgrund, where he remained for the next 16 years. He died on September 5, 1994 at the age of 87, in Echternach, Luxembourg.

Due in part to a trust established by the Mergenthalers for the upkeep of St. Mauritius, the church has been able to upgrade and keep current over the years. Today the vestibule is enclosed in glass with special lighting used to showcase the wall tribute to George. Oak benches have been replaced with padded chairs and in 1985 a new modern organ replaced the previous one.

A mile down the road from Eschweiler, marking the place near where George's body was found, stands a rough hewn gray stone monument at the head of a flat bed of slate, inscribed with a rephrasing of George's parting words to Father Bodson: *"My Father do not fear-I will defend you"*. Flowers are always present at the base of the monument. Close to the monument is a placard describing in detail, in English and in French, what happened just down the road on that fateful December day in 1944.

At the former Pletschet house is another monument of sorts. It was there that George spent much of his time while in Eschweiler, especially the last two weeks of his life, when he shared a second floor room with Cletus. To this very day, although the Pletschet family has long since moved from the house, they still refer to that room as "George's room".

The Mergenthaler Family Plot in Holy Sepulchre Cemetery, Rochester NY

AUTHOR'S POST NOTE:

In November of 2019, ahead of the 75th Anniversary of the Battle of the Bulge, George's act of selfless heroism was finally recognized by the United States Government. Congressman Eliot Engel of New York introduced into the Congressional Record (the official account of the proceedings of the US Congress) an accounting of George's too brief life and his courageous act; an act certainly deserving of the Medal of Honor.

Congressional Record

United States
of America
PROCEEDINGS AND DEBATES OF THE *116th* CONGRESS, FIRST SESSION

House of Representatives

HONORING

GEORGE MERGENTHALER

HON. ELIOT L. ENGEL
OF NEW YORK
IN THE HOUSE OF REPRESENTATIVES

Madam Speaker, as we approach the 75th Anniversary of the Battle of the Bulge, I would like to take a moment to honor a true American hero, George Mergenthaler.

George was born on August 5th, 1920 and was the only child of Alice and Hermann Mergenthaler of Rye, NY. He grew up in Rye and was later accepted into Princeton University in September of 1939.

A gifted athlete, dedicated student, handsome and charismatic, "Merg" as he was known, was well liked by all who knew him. With studies that focused on History and English, George's time at Princeton was everything he could have hoped for.

All that changed on December 7, 1941 when the Japanese bombed Pearl Harbor. Like many of his generation, George enlisted soon after the attack, but his enlistment was deferred until he graduated in January 1943 in an accelerated program. Just days later he was sent to Camp Hood in Texas for basic training. Discovering his fluency with German and French, the army assigned George to the 28th Cavalry Reconnaissance Troop.

Following overseas training in Wales, George and the rest of the Recon Troop entered the European Theater of Operation in mid-July 1944 with the 28th Infantry Division and would fight their way through France, into Belgium and on to Luxembourg. In mid-November the Troop arrived into Eschweiler, Luxembourg, their home for the next month.

Because of his ease with language, George more than any of the other soldiers, endeared himself to the people of the small farming town. Together they shared meals, church services, hopes and dreams. Then on December 16th, 1944, the Germans launched a surprise attack in the Ardennes Forest. The Battle of the Bulge was underway. By mid-afternoon on December 18th, the German attack had pushed deep into Luxembourg, and Eschweiler was nearly surrounded. The Recon Troop held the town as long as possible before pulling out. Just a mile outside of town, their convoy drove into a German ambush. Pinned down on the narrow, treelined road, death or capture were their only options. Realizing their desperate situation, George sprang to action. Showing no regard for his personal safety, George jumped into the back of a jeep, manned a .50-caliber machine gun and provided enough covering fire for the rest of the Recon Troop soldiers to make their escape. Seconds later the machine gun jammed. As George tried to clear the breach, German bullets cut him down. George's selfless and heroic actions that day allowed the rest of the Recon Troop to survive not only that ambush but the war.

Madam Speaker, George Mergenthaler made the ultimate sacrifice that day so that others could live in peace. I would like to thank this body for posthumously recognizing George Mergenthaler, a true American hero.

Later that month, in a ceremony at St. Mauritius Church, an official copy of that Congressional Record was presented to the people of Eschweiler.

Photo: Nick Malget

Through the years, the story of George Mergenthaler and the church in Eschweiler has been told in several newspaper articles and magazine features. In the course of writing this story however, it became clear that certain events or details surrounding the story were missing, incomplete or inaccurate. Many of those details, then accepted as fact, were recounted time and again, perpetuating the inaccuracies. Through painstaking research that included the gathering of information from declassified US Army After Action reports, unit records and histories, individual service records, family records, news accounts of the time, veteran memoirs, and especially multiple interviews with veterans and civilians who knew George and/or knew details surrounding various aspects of the story because they were there, I was able to piece together in "MERG" the most complete and factual telling of this story. Those who were there and lived this story deserved that.

Acknowledgements:

A true story, writing MERG would not have been possible without the help of those who embraced the project and graciously offered their help. My thanks to all (in no particular order):

Quentin LaFond and his mother Anne Lafond, for sharing Cletus' story and giving a unique perspective on George's life in the army and the close friendship that grew between the two soldiers.

Sally Ross, who happily shared her family photographs and memories of some of her distant relatives.

Seimon Pugh Jones, who helped with insight into what life was like for the soldiers when they were stationed in St. Clears, Wales.

Vic Weber, Jos Arens, Fraçois Theis, Johny Schlimm, Nicolas Lucas, Jerry Streitz, Marcel Scheidweiler, Marcel Krischler, Henri Krischler, Pit Krischler, Anna Jans-Damit, Jos Scheer and Nick Malget, who helped with the gathering of information and photographs related to war time life in Luxembourg and Eschweiler in particular.

Richard Brookins, the American St. Nicolas, who as a veteran of WWII, shared his first-hand knowledge of some of the major battles of this story as well as detailing army life at the time.

Victoria Pletschet, as well as 28th Cavalry Reconnaissance Troop veterans Charles "Chuck" Jones, Richard Sheesley and Gene McHale, all of the whom knew George personally and shared their memories of him and their experiences from the war. Thanks also to Chandra Capps Kendall for sharing her father's story.

Thanks to my wife Karen and our friends David and Lee for their patience and what I still believe was genuine interest in my telling and retelling of all or parts of this story again and again over many dinners.

About the Author:

Peter Lion is a 7-time Emmy Award winning television Producer, Director and Writer.

He is also the author of the international best selling book "American St. Nick".

A New England native, he currently resides in Connecticut with his wife and their four dogs.

For more information or to book Peter for a speaking engagement or book signing visit:

www.PeterLionAuthor.com

Printed in the USA
CPSIA information can be obtained
at www.ICGtesting.com
CBHW061909280724
12325CB00019B/575